THE START
JOURNEY TO ENTREPRENEURSHIP

Ainsley & Allen Publishing

NEWARK, DELAWARE

Ainsley & Allen Publishing LLC
2035 Sunset Lake Road
Newark, DE 19702
www.ainsleyallenpublishing.com

Ordering Information:
Quantity sales. Special discounts are available on quantity purchases by corporations, associations, and others. For details, contact the "Special Sales Department" at the address above.

The START. —1st ed.
978-0-9975855-0-6

Library of Congress Control Number: 2016955122

LEMONADE DAY

Empowering Today's Youth to Become Tomorrow's Entrepreneurs

Lemonade Day is a nation-wide educational program that empowers youth to take ownership of their lives and become productive members of society – the business leaders, social advocates, volunteers, and forward thinking citizens of tomorrow by teaching the entrepreneurial skills necessary to start, own and operate their own business... a lemonade stand.

You can learn more about Lemonade Day by visiting LemonadeDay.org

CONTENTS

INTRODUCTION

Nobody becomes an entrepreneur because it's easy.

They're driven by an unstoppable dream. It's a life calling, not a career. They hold themselves to relentlessly high standards, and when they fall, they fall hard.

Entrepreneurs who start businesses armed only with ideas and a rough plan – rather than a structured organization backed with capital, talented employees and a full stock of products – face a multitude of unique challenges. As a result, these business owners often have colorful and illuminating war stories of survival – especially from their early years.

Sometimes they make their way via trial and error, sometimes with luck, but usually it is through perseverance. And while they are happy to share their stories, most end up doing so only with friends and family. Entrepreneurs don't often get the opportunity to reach a broader audience, or indeed enlighten other businesspeople that could benefit from their wisdom and experience.

The Authority Media Group presents the remarkable findings of its study of successful entrepreneurs in "THE START."

Compiled from candid conversations with active entrepreneurs from vastly different styles and backgrounds, "THE START" allows us to discover some common and not so common traits that often go unrecognized. Sharing the defining moments in their journey to entrepreneurship, from childhood business ambitions to early work life, revealing the moment they crossed over from "I'm going to be an entrepreneur" to "I am an entrepreneur" and the reaction they received from friends and family. You'll read about the successes and failures they encountered along the way, and the lessons learned that they still apply today.

If you've ever thought about going into business for yourself, chances are you will probably recognize some of the same feelings of doubt and exhilaration described within these pages. Filled with vital performance and career lessons that you can apply to your business and life, "THE START" is a fascinating, inspirational and motivating must-read for entrepreneurs at every level.

We hope you enjoy these stories and benefit from their wisdom.

DUANE SIEBERT

THE START: Journey to Entrepreneurship

I know exactly when the entrepreneurial seed started for me – September 1967. I was twelve years old, in a band and wanted a $300 Fender Stratocaster. At the time, I had $25 to my name.

Telling my dad my "problem" he said, "The only way to get that guitar is by getting a job."

I said, "How can I get a job?"

He said, "Walk up and down Lincoln Highway after school and stop in every business and tell them you need a job. Tell them why and tell them you are willing to do whatever they need you to do and see what happens."

The first day was brutal.

The second day was a miracle.

Not only did I get a job paying $1.45 an hour, but it was also at another guitar shop, polishing guitars, cleaning up, etc. The most amazing part was I met Michael, the 19-year old who hired me.

Shortly after hiring me, he dropped out of college and opened his own "stereo store." This was big news in 1967. He took me with him as his "gopher" and grew that first store into a 15-store chain grossing more than $25 million a year.

Not only did I get my Stratocaster, but Michael also showed me entrepreneurship every day and he has been my best friend and mentor for the last 49 years!

I loved school, but I was always distracted and disruptive. If I really liked a subject, A's were no problem. Other classes only got minor attention and B's or C's would result.

When I was even younger, I had sold greeting cards as a Boy Scout and "Grit" magazine door-to-door. My only after school job was working at Michael's stereo store and my dad would not let me work there if my grades ever fell below a B average which never happened.

I did go to college for a while. My primary goal after high school, and I still don't know why, was to be a stockbroker. I did an internship at Merrill Lynch over the winter break of my sophomore year in college and that really reinforced my desire to be a stockbroker.

After dropping out of college I took a job as a junior accountant but decided I would pursue that stockbroker job. Despite the fact that I didn't have their required four-year degree, I annoyed the branch office manager at Merrill Lynch enough that he finally said, "Show up on Monday with a suit on and we'll give you a try."

CROSSING OVER:
From "I'm going to be" to "I am" an Entrepreneur

I had no way of knowing, but my firsthand entrepreneurial experience with Michael for a decade-plus had ruined me for working in corporate America. It wasn't as if I decided to become an entrepreneur so much as it was the "universe" and my bosses in the brokerage industry "helped" me decide.

Even with 10+ years of hating wearing a three-piece suit, I didn't really figure it out. Contemplating the fact I had been released (fired) from Merrill, E.F. Hutton, Smith Barney and then Merrill (one more, time – I convinced them to take me back), I started to think, "Maybe stock brokering isn't me."

As I have seen so many times in my life and the lives of others, the single best thing of my entire life happened on the heels of the worst thing. At the start of my "lost decade" of being a stockbroker I met my wife (now of 37 years), Annette. She, too, was a stockbroker at Merrill. She was great at it. I clearly stunk.

So, it took my dad laying out the "You can have anything you want by working for it!" groundwork, meeting Michael, my friend and the best entrepreneurial role model one could ever hope for, and becoming a stockbroker and getting fired multiple times to finally get me close to jumping off the entrepreneurial cliff.

Giving credit where it is due, I was still looking for a "job." Annette was the one who said, "I don't think working for someone else suits you. You've talked about it, why don't you start your own business?"

That sounded like a good idea so I started my hunt to figure out what that business would be. I bought every business related magazine I could find and combed through the stories and the ads for business opportunities. Loving electronics and enjoying taking stuff apart, fixing it, reassembling it, all of that came together to make me decide on laser printer toner cartridge remanufacturing (it was 1987 and laser printers were brand new).

With nothing more than one day's training in the basement of a high school guidance counselor who was a part-time toner cartridge remanufacturer, my Merrill Lynch cold-calling training and my experiences of working on anything/everything at Michael's stereo stores, "The Laser Group" was born.

You know how it's so easy for any of us to see with perfect clarity what our friends, family members, politicians, are doing wrong, but we seem to have a really hard time doing that looking at our own lives?

That's exactly what happened when I told friends and family I was going to start my own business. Almost every one of them said some variation of, "FINALLY!" or "We told you that wearing a suit and tie, playing stockbroker wasn't for you!" They were all for it. I just wish my dad had been around to see it. He died at 49 the day before I turned 21.

LESSONS LEARNED

I got really, really lucky and my first business venture, "The Laser Group" (renamed TonerRefillKits.com in 1999) worked beyond my wildest dreams. Our 30th year in business is coming up in December 2016.

In my first year, I had gross revenues just shy of $30,000 working from our townhouse basement, in my bathrobe, watching Andy Griffith reruns, with my trusty Sheltie, "Winky", at my side.

Life was good. Annette was still a full-time stockbroker making nearly $150,000 annually. I was the master of my "The Laser Group" domain… Life wasn't just good; it was freaking great!

One fateful day, Annette came home from work and over pizza, an Italian beef sandwich and beer at "Papa Pasero's" in Westmont, Illinois, she asked this seemingly innocuous question as only wives can do, "Do you ever think The Laser Group will generate enough revenue so I could work there, too?"

Not knowing what my answer was about to set in motion, I took a big swig of beer and with all of the bravado a business genius whose company grossed $30,000 and cleared maybe $10,000 can muster said, "Sure! That would be great!"

The next day Annette came home from work and said, "I did it!"

Me: "You did what?"

Annette: "I quit."

Me: "That's funny. What did you really do?"

Annette: "I quit."

Panicked and hoping she had given them like five years notice so I could keep hanging out in my bathrobe in the basement, I said, "Effective when...?"

Annette: "Immediately!"

Her "Immediately" coupled with the loss of her $150K income and her massive efforts to help me "get it", turned into $179,000 revenue in our second year, $464,000 in the third, just missing $1,000,000 the fourth.

29 years later we've sold $50+ million of toner to 100,000+ customers around the globe.

The story of Annette making great money and me working in my bathrobe highlights a really important point. Your "fire in the belly" needs to consume you. I didn't have it when we still had her income.

Only when she had the courage to step up and make it "real" by quitting her job did The Laser Group take off.

But, growing from $30,000 in year one to nearly a million in our fourth year carried with it the biggest seed of our near complete destruction.

I wasn't smart enough to slow down my prospecting or space out my advertising to control our growth. Cartridge remanufacturing required hands-on touching/handling of every single cartridge a customer sends in. I used to open the door to our one-car garage and tell Annette, "Look at all of that business!" Annette was far wiser and would say, "Look at all of those angry customers who still are waiting for their cartridges and the backlog is growing every day!"

It sounds counterintuitive, but massive, unexpected or unplanned for growth will kill your business far faster than slow, less than hoped for or planned for, growth. Even 30 years ago people wanted a quick turnaround and no matter how good your products or services, if you can't deliver they will revolt.

You can still aim for massive growth, but figure out what you are going to do when the SHTF and you have way more business than you can handle before it happens.

The biggest failure that contributed to our 30-year success is related to that unexpected growth. In our fifth year, we landed our biggest customer ever. We were remanufacturing approximately 700 cartridges per month and this new customer's first shipment was 500 cartridges.

Within a matter of months they started sending us 4,000 cartridges per month. Even 500 cartridges per month put us in the top 5% of all companies in the still new cartridge remanufacturing industry. 4,700 per month put us well into the top 1%.

Through lessons learned over the prior years we were able to accommodate that huge increase in business. We moved into new quarters, hired people we already had on our radar for future growth, etc. Everything we did was geared toward making certain our 4,000 cartridge per month customer was taken care of the best they possibly could be.

What we weren't ready for was what you do when we lost our biggest customer that represented 80% of our business.

As if I had never heard, "Don't put all your eggs in one basket"? Not only that, but, I learned the hard way you don't cater to your biggest customer and lose sight of the fact all of your other customers were the ones who made it possible for you to attract the big customer in the first place. To keep the giant customer happy, we put their cartridges at a 60% discount from our normal pricing at the front of the line and everyone else paying retail came a distant second.

When they left us for another competitor that came in $.52/cartridge lower than our price, our customer didn't tell us or give us a chance to compete. They just vanished. We were hugely over-staffed, had production capacity we didn't need, and far too much inventory for their particular cartridges. It was a disaster.

Despite focusing on nothing else for nearly a month, Annette and I were at a complete loss to figure out how to find another 4,000 cartridge per month customer. Another reality we had to face was our biggest customer found us, we didn't find them, so it wasn't something we could easily duplicate.

Our salvation finally hit me one morning in the shower, "Duh! I don't need to replace 4,000 cartridges per month, I don't even need to replace the gross revenue of that many cartridges per month, I just need to replace the profit!"

Rushing to our offices/warehouse and putting pencil to paper I was shocked to realize we only needed to bring in 275 cartridges per month. This was approximately 125 new customers at our average 2.2 cartridges per customer, per month at our normal retail prices to replace the profit we lost when our huge customer disappeared.

We knew beyond a shadow of a doubt how to find 125 small customers, and we did exactly that in under four months.

That lesson, as we have told people over the years, "Think of the pyramids in Egypt. They haven't survived for eons because they are made of one giant stone; they are made of thousands and thousands and thousands of interlocking stones. Build a business made up of thousands of customers where not a single one accounts for more than 10% of your revenue and your business is far more stable."

BACK TO THE START:
Advice to My Pre-Entrepreneur Self

Passion is hugely over-rated, in my humble opinion. If you are passionate about an industry or service that no one wants, you will have a really tough future because trying to create demand is tough.

Instead, pick a growing business/industry that has legs. In fact, competition is your friend because it tells you it is a business that enjoys huge popularity and demand, and it is far easier to carve out your niche via branding and thereby have a greater chance of success.

Now, while I said passion is over-rated, here is a great piece of advice I received several years ago from a very successful entrepreneur who is now a good friend, "Don't give up on your passions. Let your passions be the reasons you are driven to succeed in a business that offers far better chances of monetary success so you can then take that money and fund your passions instead of trying to derive income from them."

About Duane Siebert

Duane Siebert has always known he was going to be very successful in life, as long as he put his heart into it. Without going through college and getting a degree, he managed to secure a job at Merrill Lynch as a stockbroker. This is where he met the love of his life, his wife Annette, who also became his business partner. Duane saw success in everything he did. After 29 years of running his toner refill business he still does not give himself time to recharge. All his energy is spent putting every second of his time into furthering his business and becoming even more successful.

TonerRefillKits.com

WEBSITE
TonerRefillKits.com

FACEBOOK
Facebook.com/TonerRefillKits/

EMAIL
DSiebert@TonerRefillKits.com

TWITTER
@TheRefillMan

LINKEDIN
LinkedIn.com/in/DuaneKSiebert

PHONE
352-343-7533

J. NICHOLE SMITH

THE START: Journey To Entrepreneurship

Being an entrepreneur. I don't know that I ever had a choice in the matter. It's in my DNA. I was an only child. My Dad never had a "real" job, and my Mom started her own business straight out of college. I remember sitting around the table listening to my parents and their adult friends. I knew the definition of customer service at age six because that was the chat at my house.

I did all the regular teenager things like babysitting. In high school, I wedged myself into the yearbook department and sold fancy senior portrait sessions to my friends. I had to meet with the school board to get them to approve independent photos in the yearbook instead of the boring old school photos. They approved, which allowed me to capitalize on the opportunity.

I think a strong element of my personality is that I am a people pleaser. I was a very good student and got straight A's. From middle school through high school I volunteered at a veterinary clinic and thought I wanted to be a veterinarian.

I took a photography class in high school and started taking photos of the pets that were being cared for at the clinic. My boss saw some of my work and was very impressed. She asked me, "Are you sure you want to be a vet?" I assured her that I absolutely did want to be a veterinarian. I didn't want to be a starving artist. She told me, "Okay, you realize you are not going to be able to take any photography classes in college?" I said, "Sure I will. I will have electives." She said, "No. It will be math and science all the way." That was a light bulb moment for me; I don't like math or science.

I quickly looked for a job that would support my ambition and interest and was hired by the portrait studio that was shooting our senior prom. I was back in the line of work that I wanted to go into. I stayed pretty focused from there on out to be a photographer throughout college and ended up leaving college to start my own business.

CROSSING OVER:
From "I'm going to be" to "I am" an Entrepreneur

I went the university because my Mom wanted me to do a year of "real" school before I went to art school. I hated it. I got really good grades, but I was super bored. It just wasn't my thing. We had a big fight, and she told me that if I left, she would not pay for my college. I told her that was fine because I could do it myself. I left the university, applied to art school and was accepted. It was very expensive, $20,000 a year – and the year was only eight months long. I had to get student loans. My parents separated and I had to rely on Dad as my cosigner to get a student loan for my first year. When year two rolled around and I reminded him it was time for another student loan, he said, "Wait a minute. I thought that was it. I signed up. That was all."

With no money and no cosigner, I couldn't afford to go back. I wanted to finish, so I decided to transfer to a less expensive school. It was during my third year of school that I thought to myself, "Why am I paying for school when I know I can do this right now?" I could get paid for my photography instead of paying for a degree, so I left. (I did end up getting a Master's degree later). I started my business straight out of school.

I was doing an internship with a maternity photographer. She photographed pregnant women and their families. She shot with black and white film, which is a very specific niche. I discovered that having a specific niche like that was really important. While I was interning with her I had gotten a puppy and was desperately in love with the dog so she suggested, "Why not make pet photography as your niche?"

I thought she was nuts, but I started to look into it and discovered there were very few pet photographers at the time. It really captivated me. It was something I knew I could do so I made some business cards that said I was a pet photographer and ended up booking my first shoot the very next day.

About three months later I ran into a woman that wanted me to photograph her dog. As we began talking, we realized that there was a great opportunity to create a business. She was a bookkeeper and had other business skills that I didn't have. She was the brains, and I was the brawn, our talents complemented each other, so we decided to become partners.

LESSONS LEARNED

It became very complicated, very quickly. My new partner and I decided to go into a trademark licensing agreement with a brand that would require us to have a retail shop with a photo-studio element. We signed on the line for about $50,000 of inventory that we never received. They really screwed us over. I was only 20 years old, four weeks into my new business and filing a lawsuit that ended up lasting five years. It was trial by fire and a pretty crazy way to start a business.

I was very, very naïve when I started my business. I was blinded by the idea of having my own studio. I didn't do my due diligence. I relied on my partner to take care of a lot of the stuff that I didn't understand, instead of learning about it myself. Even though we hardly knew each other when we became partners, we stuck together.

After spending $60,000 on legal fees we won the lawsuit, but the other party quickly filed bankruptcy. This left us with $100,000 loss to split between the two of us. It took almost a decade to pay off the debt.

It was a very tangible lesson in starting the business. The process was incredibly stressful. I was working as hard as I could just to pay the bills and legal fees. It felt unfair, and I felt stupid for not looking further down the road.

I realized I had to make a choice. I can just quit, get a regular job and become this angry and resentful person or I can choose to believe that this is part of my journey, take what I can from it, and move on.

This was a defining moment for me. I made the shift to become much more positive and growth-oriented rather than just focused on the survival of that situation.

I feel fortunate to have had total support when I went into business. I have always been in a very lucky situation to be surrounded by entrepreneurs. My parents, their friends, other family members – so many entrepreneurs supporting me in my endeavor.

For me being an entrepreneur has, by definition, hundreds of roller coaster moments, high highs, and low lows. I don't think most entrepreneurs would have it any other way because the highs are so high. I don't know anyone who has started a business they cared about and not experienced those extremes.

I remember someone saying to me very early on, "In business, relationships are everything." I didn't quite understand what that meant at the time. Now that I have a Master's Degree in Marketing and have been in business for over a decade, I understand how being invested in building relationships is very important. It's not so much who you know, but rather it's about the relationships that you build with your peers, vendors, clients, potential clients, your community and even total strangers. I believe it's very important to build goodwill all around you by being very generous with a wealth of information and assistance.

I've met several new entrepreneurs through my consulting work who struggle with feelings of being copied or that others are stealing away their clients or customers.

BACK TO THE START:
Advice to My Pre-Entrepreneur Self

If you believe in karma—the great universal give and take—that what you give out comes back to you, then it's much harder to get distracted by competition or feelings of jealousy. If you can root yourself in the attitude of relationship building and giving, it is much easier to remain steady and focused.

About J. Nichole Smith

Nichole is one of those people who were born to be an entrepreneur. Growing up surrounded by a family of entrepreneurs pushed her to do what she was passionate about. Even when her parents pushed back and tried getting her onto a stable career path, Nichole did her own thing. Today she is the owner of *Working with Dog,* a site that helps people learn about marketing for their pet stores. She also does one-on-one meetings to advance her clients' businesses by giving them all the tools they need.

One of the main reasons Nichole created her business was so she could travel the world. At the time of her interview, she and her husband were in France, living each moment to the fullest.

I run a community called "Working with Dog." It's a membership site that I've built for petpreneurs that focuses on coaching and delivering content. We have an incredible community on Facebook. It's an incredibly supportive place centered around marketing, so helping small businesses grow, in a way that I'm not able to do one-to-one because I'm too expensive for most of the petpreneurs who need me. I wanted a way to be able to help everyone, in a way that speaks to me as well, so that I can have the lifestyle that I want.

My time is split between creating content, either myself or curating with pet or marketing experts. I'm writing a book at the moment, called "The Million Dollar Dog Brand," which is based on interviews with 10 of the most amazing, inspirational, pioneer petpreneurs who started 10, 15 years ago, some really great brands like *Bark Off* and *Ruffwear*. Then I spend a good deal of time doing one-on-one, online group, and corporate consulting.

I continue to build my platform as an authority in order to build the awareness for the community that I've created. I'm really passionate about the pet industry and helping businesses operate more like brands and really be able to do what I've done in terms of taking what they're best at and giving it back in a way that people stand up and take notice.

Working with Dog

WEBSITE
WorkingWithDog.com

FACEBOOK
Facebook.com/WorkingWithDog

EMAIL
hello@dane-dane.com

TWITTER
@workingwithdog

LINKEDIN
UK.LinkedIn.com/in/JNichole

INSTAGRAM
@workingwithdog

MATT TRAINER

THE START: Journey To Entrepreneurship

I grew up in an extremely poor family, but from the time I was about three years old I knew that I was going to be a very successful person. I know you don't understand much at that age, and I didn't know how it was going to happen, but I knew.

Very early on I started several businesses, the typical lemonade stand, snow shoveling, and lawn mowing. I didn't completely grasp that I was a full-on entrepreneur even when I was in high school. I thought I was going to be an engineer.

I had great grades in school, but it wasn't because I tried very hard. I probably could have been at the very top of the class, except I didn't want to be part of the system. I was always thinking outside the box, leading my little silent rebellions and figuring out ways to get around doing homework.

I always did well on tests even though I didn't study. That would get me in trouble with my teachers because they thought I was cheating. I wasn't. I just had the gift of a good memory, and I understood the material quickly.

You could call my father a career student. He has six or seven college degrees and a couple of Master's degrees, but he really never applied anything. When I did well on my SAT's and snagged a bunch of scholarships, he sat me down and said, "You might be better off if you do not go to school. Take a couple of years and work in the engineering field as an apprentice or something, and then go to school. You'll learn a lot more than being in school and may find out you like it better." This was shocking to me coming from a man who spent his life going to school.

I did want to be an engineer, so at the age of eighteen I took his advice and got a job with an engineering company. Within a few years, I was running the entire company. There were guys that had kids my age and had been working there for twenty plus years; yet I was their boss because I was better at it.

I never went back to school. Instead, I started an engineering company along with a lot of other businesses.

CROSSING OVER:
From "I'm going to be" to "I am" an Entrepreneur

There I was, in my early twenties, running the engineering company and I felt tapped out. I knew I wasn't going anywhere. A few times a year we would hire consultants to come in to meet with us on whatever projects we had going. These guys would fly in for a couple of days, help us work on cool stuff, and then fly out.

This intrigued me because at that time I had never really traveled anywhere in my life. I started asking them what they did and learning how they had setup their businesses as independent contractors. I liked the idea that they got to pick and choose what they wanted to do. So I decided to branch out and start a consulting firm. It was tough.

Remember when you were a little kid? How easy it was to be fearless when your parents were taking care of your food and a place to sleep. When you're all grown up and have real responsibilities, leaving a well-paying job to start your own business is scary. I'll be the first to admit that I was scared. It was rocky for a couple of years, but I got through it and learned a lot of lessons later on for other businesses.

My entire family thought I was nuts and they still do. I don't really talk to any of them anymore. I'm so much different than them. They're all wage slaves and work in cubicles, unhappy with their lives, and here I am a successful person. They always say things like, "Matt's so lucky." It's not about luck at all. They always saw me kind of as an alien. I always kind of felt that way too, which was not fun for the longest time. I always wondered, "Why do I think differently than everybody around me?"

LESSONS LEARNED

That first consulting business didn't end up going well. It started okay for a few months, maybe a year. It's a good thing I did it when I was young, dumb and fearless because it probably would have ruined me now.

But I did learn one big lesson: *Marketing is Everything*. I didn't realize that I was good at marketing until many years later.

To launch my business, I had contacted a list of companies in the industry by sending them a sales letter. This was pre-Internet days, I physically wrote the letter, hand-addressed and stamped the envelopes, and mailed out a few hundred to businesses offering my consulting services. The entire letter explained how the industry was dirty with consultants who lied and charged them for all these hours to just sit around and do nothing. I opened the lid on the industry, which was great at first; it got me a lot of business. But ultimately it was the reason I failed. I was blackballed from the industry.

Well-connected people that had been around the industry for decades longer than me put out the word "Do not work with this guy." They felt I publically exposed their dirty laundry to the industry, so they made sure I wasn't in it anymore. That kind of blackballing would not work on me today because I have connections, but back then I was just a young rebel.

That whole thing taught me to be fearless, but it also taught me to pay attention and maybe not to be so aggressive with the marketing when you're not in the power position.

I've learned to be less aggressive over the years. I pause and think about my communications before I fire them off. No matter what it's about or what method I am going to use to send it, before I do anything, I sit and think about it from all levels.

Even though I knew I was going to be successful when I was a kid, I had no idea it would feel like this. My life is better than I ever imagined it would be. I grew up in an extremely poor neighborhood now I live in an extremely wealthy neighborhood. I get to drive the cars I want to drive and travel the way I want to travel. The work I do is what I enjoy doing. It just feels like a miracle. I really feel that way and honestly believe it. My wife and I talk about it all the time; it's like we are living a dream. Now that we are in that mindset it's like everything naturally happens. You can get in miracle creation mode, and you can stay there, it is awesome.

BACK TO THE START:
Advice to My Pre-Entrepreneur Self

Listen to yourself! I think we all internally know what to do, and we are constantly seeking out more and more people for those answers. The older I get, the more I dig into myself, learn more about myself. Be brave. Don't give up.

About Matt Trainer

Matt Trainer's company is on the cutting edge for healthy organic anti-aging cream. They focus on what will benefit the customer and not what will make the most money. They are producing a cream that breathes through the skin.

Matt continues to use his marketing knowledge as a consultant for corporate clients by teaching them the best way to get their message out there and having it stick with their audience.

While Matt doesn't view his job as "work" he still uses meditation to recharge from a rough workweek. Every Sunday Matt can be found golfing. He turns off his phone so he can be by himself and enjoy the activity.

The Trainer Method

WEBSITE
MattTrainer.com

FACEBOOK
Facebook.com/TheMattTrainer

EMAIL
matt@theatlasalliance.com

TWITTER
@thematttrainer

PHONE
562-253-9445

INSTAGRAM
@thematttrainer

THE START: Journey To Entrepreneurship

I've had the entrepreneur spirit within me all my life. My parents have owned a tree business for the past 30 years. Growing up in a household of entrepreneurs, knowing if my parents weren't getting customers for their business, we didn't have money! That was a big influence on me.

My mom left her job to stay at home and take care of me. She would just answer the phone while my dad was the arborist working with the trees.

Business was slow when I was a baby, so I got that time with my family and to bond with my mom.

As I grew so did the business. By the age of 10, I saw my mom become a certified arborist – she is one of the few women in the field. My dad is certified as well.

When I was about six, my friend across the street and I would start businesses on the block selling little creative projects like painted rocks. I think my mom's favorite were the bags of water that we added glitter in to make the sparkly. We would sell them for $0.50 or $50. We let our customers pick their price, but I wouldn't recommend that as a business model.

We also sold silly things like chalk dust. There was a little niche market that I tapped into as a 6-year-old little ballerina. We would scrape up and bag the chalk along the cement and try to sell it to my ballerina friends as a way to make the Rosin on their dance shoes more colorful.

I was pretty much an A/B student and involved in tons of activities. I still have a problem volunteering for more than I can handle. In the tenth grade I was in the drama club and single-handedly wrote, directed, and produced the Christmas program for the entire school. I was also a commissioner of public relations for my drama club.

I ran for class president four times and never won, but I wouldn't give up. I did, however, win Drama Club president my senior year. I was a very persistent child.

I was dead set on working in Hollywood as an actress and a writer, and as anyone in Hollywood will tell you, that takes a ton of entrepreneurial hustle. As a teenager I struggled with perfectionism. I was incredibly hard on myself. It's something I still struggle with today. A little perfectionism goes a long way, but too much can hinder your projects from being finished as well as prevent anything else from being started. There are always perfect ideas in your head, but once you bring them into the world of reality, sometimes they don't turn out exactly as you expected.

My senior year of high school, I put so much pressure on myself to go to college. That was the next step in life. I was so depressed because I was taking AP courses, college classes, honors courses and I was driving myself crazy.

I remember the day my mom was dropping me off at school, and she turned to me and said, "Kim. You want to be an actress and a writer. You want to be working. You don't need college. You don't even need the advanced classes that you're taking. No one cares in Hollywood. If you need to drop out because this is so taxing for you, you're stressing yourself out way too much and just start pursuing your dreams. I will support that to get you out of the depression." That was such a huge relief and made me realize that the only one putting pressure on myself was myself.

CROSSING OVER:
From "I'm going to be" to "I am" an Entrepreneur

I was accepted to and was going to attend a conservatory because I had two scholarships. Two weeks before I was supposed to start, I looked at my mom and said, "You know what? I think I want to start working. I want to figure out what fields I want to focus on, I want to write, and I want to pursue my dream career."

My parents were incredibly supportive and understanding. They said, "You're a hard worker. We'll take the money that we've saved for your college, and you can use that to join networking groups and take classes and gain mentors and do internships for four years, the time that you would've been at school. After four years, you must get a job and move out or start paying rent, but we will support you in pursuing this dream like we would have supported you to go to college."

That was our agreement and all I needed to get going. Being a very independent and impatient person, I shortened the timeline and within two years, I had started working as a Pilates instructor and moved out.

My extended family was not as supportive because they had a more traditional view and lifestyle. That included growing up, going to college, getting a good job and working your way up the ladder of success. That was not the way I saw the world.

I started joining networking groups, I was taking classes, and I was interning at different jobs to explore different career paths before I decided which path I wanted to follow. Being multi-passionate meant I had a lot of options.

I started as a script reader for a production company. For three months I read script after script, most of them were very poorly written. I was shocked at some of the stars that were attached to these films. I think I only found one or two that I highly recommended. This just inspired me to write my own.

I remember the moment a friend sat me down to talk about me being an associate producer for a film that he wanted to do. I asked if he had a script and he said no, so I said, "Well, let me write one for you," and he said, "Oh. You write?" I said, "Well, now I do."

The director and I co-wrote my first film called Bro'. It starred Danny Trejo from Machete and Spy Kids. That was a three-year process to get it written, produced, shot, edited, and then distributed by Lionsgate. In 2012, it came out internationally on Netflix.

I'm currently launching my new business, Crown Yourself Enterprises, which is a lifestyle enchantment brand. It's helping young women get a body and life that rules. I'm combining my love for storytelling and my love for health and fitness into one big sparkly disco ball of feminine delight.

I'm really excited to share with young women who are struggling with self-confidence and body image issues and healthy eating. I want to help them grow and gain the confidence they need to step authentically into their lives and their roles as women, as business owners, even as employees and to stop holding themselves back just because of fear.

LESSONS LEARNED

After becoming an entrepreneur, I realized most things in business are counterintuitive.

I learned to choose your partners wisely. I had met my script writing partner at a networking event a couple of years before we worked together. We had established a great relationship as friends over the years and worked well together.

Unfortunately, I did not take that lesson into my first online business that sold a back rehabilitation device. I was an executive for a national company. I didn't really know the person I partnered with when we launched the business. I was so excited about the product that I jumped in without paying attention to the signals that hinted we might not be a good fit as partners. It did not turn out well.

You want a partner who aligns with your values. For me, that meant someone who was as ambitious, optimistic, proactive, and passionate as I was. It needed to be someone who continually wanted to learn and improve their skillset. You can't just assume a partner is like you, or even has the same world view as you. You need to carefully vet a person, especially before you partner with anyone. I think one of the biggest things with all my entrepreneurial adventures that I have learned is you have to jump in with both feet and say, "I'll figure it out," instead of saying, "I don't know." As soon as you say I don't know, that cuts off all possibilities.

BACK TO THE START:
Advice to My Pre-Entrepreneur Self

Surround yourself with cheerleaders, mentors who inspire you, friends who encourage you, books that enlighten and challenge you to grow and become better.

You can have it all if you don't do it all yourself. Delegating is huge. You want everyone on your team to align themselves with values that you want to bring to the world.

About Kimberly Spencer

Kimberly Spencer is living her dream as a multi-passionate entrepreneur and writer. Coming from a family of entrepreneurs, it was quite easy to see that she was going to follow in their footsteps. Deciding that college life was not for her she pursued her dream. Since BRO', owning a Pilates studio and being the executive of a national online company, Kimberly has launched Crown Yourself Enterprises, combining her love of fitness and entertainment, to help girls create a body and life that rules. Her first crowned book, *Mindful Meals: How to Eat Like a Queen and Still Look Like a Princess* debuts later this year.

She spends her free time traveling with the love of her life. Together they enjoy experiencing different cultures and discovering new ideas for their businesses. When Kimberly is not writing, she also enjoys painting and listening to classical music.

Crown Yourself Enterprises

WEBSITE
CrownYourself.com

FACEBOOK
Facebook.com/CrownYourselfNow

EMAIL
info@crownyourself.com

TWITTER
@CrownYouNow

INSTAGRAM
@crownyourself.now

HANS RIJFKOGEL

THE START: Journey To Entrepreneurship

I was always trying to do some type of business when I was young. I started by collecting old paper, buying and selling things, just trying to make a profit. By the time I was 12 or 13 years old I knew I wanted to set up my own company.

My first job after university was with a food company that sold vegetable and animal oils and fats. I lived in England for a while doing their sales in the United Kingdom and got to travel around Europe.

Next, I went to work for Holland-based Agio Cigars for 17 years, handling their export business in parts of Europe, the Middle East, Asia, and Eastern Europe.

CROSSING OVER:
From "I'm going to be" to "I am" an Entrepreneur

1n 2013, I decided there were three things I was looking for in my life. I wanted to continue working for Agio Cigars, I wanted to move back to Asia, and I wanted to set up my own company.

I'm not somebody who goes into one business after another and tries a million things. I have to think about it and then if I feel that it is something for me, then I'll go into it. But it's not done on impulse. I like being in the cigar world, and the cigar business, so I tried to combine all those things together. After several months of figuring out the best way to handle it I thought, "If I'm not going to do it now, I am probably never going to do it."

So I went to Agio Cigars and told them that I would love to continue working with them, but I wanted to go back to Asia because there are so many opportunities there. I presented them with the idea for me to handle their sales and marketing in Asia and after some discussion, they agreed. I am now based in Taiwan, in the city of Taipei.

About a year ago, I was approached by an American company, Swisher Cigars, asking me to handle their sales in Asia. Now I have three companies, Agio Cigars, Swisher, and Drew Estate, for which I handle all their sales in Asia.

Most of my friends and family supported me. Some of them knew that I had always wanted to set up my own company, so it was not a complete surprise. To most of my colleagues and friends, it was a surprise that I was going to set up my own company in a completely different part of the world. They offered help if I needed it, but nobody told me "You are out of your mind."

I started my company three years ago, and I'm very happy with it. I have the freedom to do what I like. I can make my own decisions. If I think something is a good idea, then I can go for it. I do not have a boss or manager telling me that I cannot do something. I can make my own destiny.

LESSONS LEARNED

It's a lot of hard work. This is not always a bad thing but when you own the company, there is a tendency to work a lot more. I love what I am doing so I don't mind working extra hours.

You do become sort of a one-man show, having to do everything yourself. When you're working for a big company, there are a lot of different departments: Finance, Sales, Computer, etc. When you're on your own you become all those departments. While working for Agio Cigars, if something were wrong with my computer I would call the IT department and say, "There's something wrong. Can you come over?" They would arrive in five minutes and would fix whatever was wrong. Now, I have to figure it out myself.

I've learned that you have to take it one step at a time. You can't do everything at once. As long as you keep going, get assistance, know where you are and where you want to go, then you will know what you have to do to achieve your goal.

While some people may disagree, for me there are no shortcuts. You have to follow your plan and keep working at it. Be persistent. In the end, you will be successful.

During the last 20 or 30 years, I have tried out a lot of different things business-wise, more like a part-time entrepreneur, not like a full-time entrepreneur. I learned what I would like to do and which areas I would like to work in. I also learned where I did not want to work. I try to do that now, to be in the right environment, to work with the right product, to work with the right people, to make a mix of those items and see if that works. For now, it does, so I am very happy.

BACK TO THE START:
Advice to My Pre-Entrepreneur Self

Prepare yourself. Preparation is extremely important, you cannot know exactly what is going to happen, but know what you want to do. Plan ahead. The other thing I would recommend is to do what you love to do. Follow your passion.

If you set up a business and it is not something that you really like doing every day, I am not sure if it will ever be a success. I do not think that is going to work. Do something that you love doing, make a good plan, prepare and then go for it.

About Hans Rijfkogel

Hans Rijfkogel currently runs his own marketing and sales agency. He gives advice to duty-free operators and importers in Asia. He also talks to different businesses around the world about the cigars they would like to have sold all over Asia.

Hans is a sincere man, doing what he is passionate about and never giving up. After working for a cigar company for many years, he was able to branch off to start his own company distributing cigars in Asia, and he was even able to keep his old employer as a client. While Hans no longer plays soccer, he is still an avid watcher of the sport. He enjoys golfing on the weekends to recharge from a strenuous work week.

Asia Marketing Services

WEBSITE
AsiaMarketingServices.com

FACEBOOK
Facebook.com/Hans.Rijfkogel.1

LINKEDIN
LinkedIn.com/in/Rijfkogel

TWITTER
@hans_rijfkogel

INSTAGRAM
hans.rijfkogel

COURTNEY KOSTELECKY

THE START: Journey To Entrepreneurship

My entire family has been all about self-employment. My mom owned a clothing store that my grandmother started in a small town back in 1941. My dad, who played professional football with the Detroit Lions at one time, had his own business as a barber along with a couple of other ventures including a movie theater.

I did the traditional things, lemonade stand, snow cones, the typical stuff that kids do. I had a lot of fun setting up and running a neighborhood carnival. The neighborhood kids would toss checkers into mom's muffin tins, and if they hit the mark, they won a prize.

A friend of mine and I had the idea to go around town and offer to paint house numbers on the curbs. Our selling point was that it makes your place easier to find for the pizza guy and emergency responders. Obviously, if your house is on fire, it's pretty easy to find that one.

We got some cardboard stencils and a can of paint at Woolworth's department store and started selling. We charged five dollars a house, which was pretty cheap. I think we ended up making $200 or $300 in a weekend. I learned you could make a lot of money fast by selling stuff.

There was a downside. We weren't doing anything illegal because it's just painting on the curb. But, the city found out what we were doing and about three weeks later, every single house got a letter in the mail saying, "In order to improve safety, etc., if you would like the numbers painted on your house, you can have it done ..." I think they were charging 10 or 15 bucks.

Brought down by the man. But my buddy and I, we still made a couple of hundred bucks that weekend.

When I was in high school, I decided that I should hunker down for grades. I wasn't a bad kid or anything like that; I just simply did not care for school. I always had good grades for the most part, and when I applied myself, I made the honor roll.

I thought I wanted to be CEO of a Fortune 500 company, but I realized later on in life that kind of structure is a pain. It kills the entrepreneurial spirit.

Magic was a big hobby of mine growing up and I wanted to be a magician. That was my dream. I didn't want to be a part-time birthday guy, although I did some of those. I wanted to make a living as a professional magician.

I wanted to wake up in the morning, have my cup of coffee, practice my craft, sell stuff, and perform. I was fortunate enough to be able to do that for almost six years. It got really hard being on the road eight or nine months out of the year. I began looking at where I was in life. If I wanted to have any type of relationship I knew that not many women were going to say, "Hey, it's okay. Have fun. We'll see you in a few months when you come back."

I worked for Wal-Mart for several years and made a lot of good friends, but I also got a little bit complacent because of the steady paycheck. It was good for me because I needed that change in my life at that time but when my seven-year tenure came up, I was out of there.

I sold cell phones for a while. I sold educational software. I worked for Yahoo selling PPC advertising. They had a small division located in North Dakota where I was living at the time. I sold a PPC campaign to the Trump Organization. I worked for Microsoft doing inside sales.

I got downsized from Microsoft, but I was able to go work for another guy who was doing the same thing that I was doing at Microsoft, basically doing regeneration for Microsoft partners selling the high-end CRM systems. While the security is nice knowing that you've got money coming in every Friday, I just like being an entrepreneur, in charge of my destiny. If you structure your business properly, you can still have that same security and even more.

CROSSING OVER:
From "I'm going to be" to "I am" an Entrepreneur

After about a year and a half, I just got tired of working for somebody. It was Christmas time; I was sitting down doing the standard, "What are you going to do for the next year" type of thing and I decided that I wanted to start my own business.

Tax time rolled around, and I had a $1,500 refund coming. Once my refund check came, I gave my two weeks' notice and told my boss, "Hey dude, I just can't do this anymore."

I had my regular paycheck, my tax refund, and knew I would be getting a final paycheck in two weeks. With a little bit of cushion I cut back my expenses to next to nothing.

I had enough money saved up to give me 60 days to land my first client. I said, "Here we go. I have a 60-day cushion. Sink or swim, baby. Sink or swim." That was the beginning of my company, Presto Marketing Group.

My mom and dad were very supportive. My boss, whose company I just left, was supportive. He's a great guy and still one of my closest friends. He became a client of mine later on. I got a lot of support from my friends, too. They knew that I was always doing something, trying to learn, trying to better myself. They knew that it was something I had always done. They were like, "Hey, yeah. Congratulations. Go for it, man."

Being Courtney today is awesome. I am blessed to be able to serve my clients from Puerto Rico and the Caribbean. I start my typical morning by grabbing a cup of coffee and going to the beach.

LESSONS LEARNED

I had my 60-day cushion. It would have been nice to have a little bit more but I think that would have made me a little bit more complacent. Even though I was out there networking, it came to a point where I was short on rent. It was due the next day and I had a meeting with a chiropractor. I knew that I had to come up with a service offering that he couldn't say no to, and not only that, but he couldn't say, "That's a lot of money. Let me think about it." I needed money today because the rent was due tomorrow.

I landed the client, but I had to give him a really, really great deal because I needed to take price out of the equation. The takeaway for me was: If you can help it, try not to sell when your back is up against the wall.

A big lesson for me was on managing the outcome of a project and client's expectations.

I was doing video marketing for this guy and I tripled his website traffic in the first 90 days of the project. It's not that he wasn't getting calls. The problem was he thought they were wasting his time, just asking questions. He didn't do any follow-up and didn't capture email addresses, so it wasn't translating into sales for him.

You can do as much as you can. You can increase traffic to the website, but it's still up to the business owner to convert that traffic into business. If they can't convert the traffic into business, they think that you didn't do your job even though you did.

I learned that you need multiple streams of income. You just can't put all your eggs in one basket. I know of a lot of companies that have one big client that they rely on. If something happens in that company's internal structure, it can upset your workflow. I try to have multiple streams of income with multiple clients.

Another thing that I learned is the power of picking a niche and serving that niche as much as you possibly can. I have an affinity for working with chiropractors. I love chiropractors, and I believe they do good work for the most part but they really need help with their marketing.

When I wrote my first book, "Chiropractor Marketing Secrets: Proven Tips, Tricks and Strategies to Get More Patients," I could have taken that same book and made it "Plumbing Marketing Secrets: How to Get More Plumbing Customers." Marketing is marketing is marketing right? I picked chiropractic because when I was a little boy a chiropractor saved my life and in my early 30s a chiropractor saved me from a very expensive knee surgery.

One of my pet peeves is a lot of marketers; they go after the chiropractors just because they're doctors, and they think they have a lot of money. My advice to somebody who is starting out as an entrepreneur is to find a tribe or a segment to serve that you feel an affinity for.

If a business comes to me outside of my chiropractic niche, and if I think I can serve them and do a good job, I will, but chiropractic is my specialty.

BACK TO THE START:
Advice to My Pre-Entrepreneur Self

Focus and balance work with your personal life and create multiple streams of income to relieve stress.

About Courtney Kostelecky

Courtney Kostelecky is a blessed individual who lives each day to the fullest. He never has a bad view and enjoys a refreshing cup of coffee each morning on the beach while he plans his day. Puerto Rico is his home and he loves going on hiking trips through the rainforest, having cookouts, traipsing around Old San Juan, or just relaxing with a picnic on the beach.

He is the best-selling author of *Chiropractor Marketing Secrets: Proven Tips, Tricks and Strategies to Get More Patients* and the upcoming book, *Seeing Stars... How to Grow Your Business With Your 5 Star Reputation.*

His website offers free tips on how to successfully market your current business.

Presto Marketing Group/Courtney Kostelecky

WEBSITE
CourtneyKostelecky.com

PHONE
701-541-1774

EMAIL
ck@courtneykostelecky.com

LINKEDIN
LinkedIn.com/in/Courtney-Kostelecky-050ab435

THE START: Journey To Entrepreneurship

Yes, it really did start out when I was a child. I grew up in a single-parent home with my mother, and we didn't have a whole lot of money. When I was in third grade, I saved up some money and put an ad in our local newspaper offering to mow yards, as long as they had a lawnmower for me to use. I was able to get eight yards that summer. Most of them were widows. I was a success. I brought in quite a bit of money riding my bike around our little town and mowing yards. It also got me started on that entrepreneurial path.

Money was tight, but I was able to do okay enough in school to get a partial scholarship to study engineering at Ohio State University.

After graduation, I started my career in the engineering field. I was able to catch on pretty quickly to various jobs and got a lot of opportunities to advance over the next ten years.

During that time I worked for a few Fortune 500 companies, moving around the country, making good money and getting assignments that most people would die for but I found myself growing dissatisfied.

I started looking outside of Corporate America for a place make my mark. I was newly married and my father-in-law, who had left Corporate America, was investing in real estate. He took me along to a few seminars, and I was considering a career switch to real estate. It was at these real estate investment seminars that I was introduced to something that caught my attention: the financial markets.

Meanwhile, I was following the corporate mindset, climbing the company ladder and moving everywhere they wanted me to move. I had pulled myself away from my family.

My wife and I were living in Texas when my mother, who lived in Ohio, got sick. We couldn't get back and forth to help out as much as we wanted, but I was able to go see her when she was in the hospital. While I was there, I helped her manage her finances and was able to relieve some of her stress. Unfortunately, she passed away when I went back to Texas. My mother didn't live long enough to see my son born.

That was traumatic. The experience made me think, "You know, I need to have more flexibility in my life. I need to have more freedom. I want to live where I want to live."

That pushed me over the edge to pursue an opportunity that I could be passionate about. I took a job that would get us back to Ohio and ended up working for that company a couple of years, but my burning desire continued to grow. During that time I started setting myself up for the transition into entrepreneurship. Part of the "getting ready" process for me included doing some things like debt consolidation and working on our finances to reduce our family overhead.

CROSSING OVER:
From "I'm going to be" to "I am" an Entrepreneur

When it ultimately came time to make the decision, I pretty much just stepped away from Corporate America. I took the Viking approach and burned the boat. I figured if I was going to make it, I needed to be 100% committed. I was 33 years old and looking at it from the standpoint that I was young enough, smart enough; I had been able to get and succeed at those jobs. It was time.

With our nest egg, a little seed money from my wife's grandparents, and our faith, we started my trading business.

A lot of people thought I was nuts. Even though some were questioning my sanity, they also provided encouragement. My wife's family, my grandparents, and even my boss, all wished us the best of luck and offered support.

My wife and I had been married for five years and had three children all under the age of three. I wasn't worried about failure. I figured it would be another chapter in my life. We would move on.

Every other Saturday, I would go to a Panera's Bread Shop in Dayton, Ohio and spent about four hours teaching people everything I knew about the financial market. Panera's let us use their meeting room as long as everybody was buying food and I was educating them for free. This went on for almost a year when my wife and I decided to move to the Carolinas and start trading 100% of my own money. As we were preparing our move, all of the people that were coming to my free Panera meetups asked, "What are we going to do when you are gone? Can you take some of this information and put it in a manual for us?"

That's how it started. Putting the system and techniques that I was teaching at those free meetings into an educational e-book created my first online product.

I put up a website to sell the e-book, and all of my old Panera students were my first customers. Not too long after the e-book success people began to ask, "Hey, can we watch you implement this process live?" The e-book evolved into what I called a live trading room where my customers could follow along and watch as I explained what I saw in the markets and how I was implementing my trading plan.

People started coming from all over to live seminars we held at a hotel in Charlotte, North Carolina. After spending the weekend watching me do live demonstrations they would ask, "Hey, is there a tool that we can have?"

From that, I developed the set of tools that has become our business today. It all came from that very humble beginning of providing free education. Prospects turned into customers. The process created a chain reaction, and we kept providing more and more value, which in turn built loyalty, as our customers started using our tools to experience their own successes.

They wanted more, we listened and continued to develop products for them. Through that I came up with what I call my "11 Pillars for Success".

LESSONS LEARNED

First and foremost, are relationships; without having a strong understanding of your customer you can't build a relationship and serve them.

It's important to spend some time developing an avatar of your ideal customer, no matter what the business is but especially if it's online.

Get detailed. He's a married male, age 29, from a middle-income family. You need to develop what that ideal customer looks like so you can be very focused as you are develop your business, your product, and your target market so you know how to advertise to get what it is you want for a customer.

I've created products and tools I thought were the greatest thing since sliced bread. I did developmental work and paid programmers only to find out my target customer didn't see the need.

I believe if you do not have failures then you're not pushing forward, but you have to learn from those failures. While developing this new tool, I would bring it up and put it in front of my customers when it was in beta form. I would ask, "What do you like about it? What do you not like about it? What's working well here? What do you think about this signal? Do we need audio?"

This time, I was not going down the road on my own, thinking I was developing everything the customer wanted only to miss the point. I wanted direct feedback.

BACK TO THE START:
Advice to My Pre-Entrepreneur Self

Make sure whatever it is you do, work your passion. You can justify the long hours, the pain, the suffering, and everything that you feel, and the success will be that much sweeter. If you are not doing it in an area that you are passionate about, whatever that may be, it's going to be very hard to have success.

Matt Brown's Eleven Pillars for Success

1. Relationships. Relate to your customers

2. Share knowledge and collaborate

3. Keep your moral compass, ignore the online haters

4. Be humble, don't run from the truth

5. Recognize success of those around you, ask for their input and guidance

6. Work in your passion

7. Don't sugarcoat issues, give it to them straight

8. Just do it, don't procrastinate

9. Be willing to fail

10. Develop your niche; you can't be everything to everyone

11. Over deliver on value

About Matt Brown

Matt Brown has and always will be a businessman. Matt puts all of his effort into making sure his customers are satisfied and that the methods he teaches are the best in the business. One of the most beneficial things that Matt has found with running his own business is having the flexibility to be a businessman and a family man. Having three kids who are all involved in different activities ranging from track to golf to swimming. Physical activities are not the only thing that Matt does with his family; they also take a couple weeks off a year to rejuvenate.

Matt Brown is not only an entrepreneur, but also an innovator. He took what he learned from years of experience and condensed it into a course that will help jump-start any beginner looking to get into the financial market. With his innovative software and unique teaching style, he has helped hundreds to leave the corporate world and become their own boss.

Following his *11 Pillars for Success,* anyone with enough dedication and hard work can make it in the financial market world!

Matt makes sure to have a good balance with faith, family and friends. Working from before the sun is even up gives Matt the afternoons to relax and spend time with the family and friends.

www.Newbie-Trader.com

WEBSITE
Newbie-Trader.com

FACEBOOK
Facebook.com/NewbieTraders

EMAIL
Admin@Newbie-Trader.com

TWITTER
@newbietraders

LINKEDIN
LinkedIn.com/in/
MattBrownTradingMentor

PHONE
888-622-6924

THE START: Journey to Entrepreneurship

As a kid I loved infomercials. I could not get enough of seeing how all the TV pitchmen were selling their products and services. I loved watching Don Lapre sell his "Make Money with Small Ads" infomercials.

I was one of those weird kids who would sign up for email lists to see what I would get. I was probably one of the only people who enjoyed being sold to; it was interesting and exciting. I wanted to reverse engineer everything and see how it worked. Everybody thought I was crazy, but it was what I liked.

I feel like I was always an entrepreneur because it's all I have done. I started on the Internet when I was 14 in a little two-bedroom apartment. In spite of medical issues, my mother worked two or three jobs. I didn't think it was fair that somebody worked so hard and not make a lot of money.

Marketing and business have kind of been my life. I guess I was just a kid who thought, "If you're going to work hard you might as well make a lot of money doing it." I didn't know I would be doing what I am doing today, but I knew it would be something to do with marketing, without a doubt.

My dad always told me he wanted me to be better than him, not like him. My parents were divorced my whole life and when my mom remarried we got our first computer back in the AOL CD Internet days. I was really into playing video games like Rollercoaster Tycoon because they were about business and making money.

CROSSING OVER:
From "I'm going to be" to "I am" an Entrepreneur

The defining moment for me was when I received my first spam email message. I know this sounds crazy, but it was exciting to get an email at that age and just getting online. I felt like I was behind all the kids in school and getting an email was something cool.

It all started with that Don Lapre Infomercial. That's what made me go on the Internet and start searching for "make money online." Only a few things popped up, but I signed up for all the newsletters. One day I got a message about a package of e-Books (at the time, I had no idea what an e-Book was). If you purchased the package, you got the rights to resell the package as well.

I opened it and the sales page was hypey, but I could not stop reading. I thought, "Wow, that's amazing!" Then I started to think, "Well, what in the world is an e-Book and who in the world would buy one?" Since there were no PDF documents back then, an e-Book was this little software program that enabled you to read the file on your computer. This offer gave you the right resell the e-Book package.

So I got the entrepreneurial bug, and it led me on the course of signing up for a bunch of newsletters. I started getting a lot of emails selling information products. I wanted this stuff so bad. I know I shouldn't have done this and it sounds horrible, but I was desperate to know the information. So, when I discovered that every marketer on the planet back then was naming their download pages "thankyou.html", I would go to their websites and add the thankyou.html to the URL, and suddenly I had access to the information.

From there, I spent hours and hours every single day on the computer, reading information, signing up for all the different free programs. It got the point that my family told me, "It's a scam. Get off it."

My life changed when I got a paper route and asked my Grandmother, "If I give you some of my money, will you put it in your bank account and let me use your credit card?" That's how I got my first domain name and my first email list. From there, everything spawned into this crazy marketing kid and where I am today.

My family was upset with me spending so much time on the computer and they kept telling me, "Get off of that thing. Quit spending all your time on the computer. Go outside and play, hang out with your friends." Our circumstances were that we had very little money, so I didn't hang out with friends a lot because I felt so driven to make money.

I obviously didn't know what I was doing and was very naïve, but I had drive. No matter what anybody said, no matter how much something didn't work for me, I kept going. I think when you are young and you fail, it is easier to keep going. It's easier to say, "Oh, that didn't work, let's do the next thing."

Eventually, my parents found out that my grandmother was taking my money and letting me use her credit card, and they were not happy about it. However, a couple of weeks later, I received my first check. It was on the same day that I had to go with my stepdad to the unemployment office. We get to the unemployment office, and the whole time he's smiling and laughing, so I asked, "Why are you acting weird?" He said, "Well, I'm going to the unemployment line and you're making money, and you're not even at the computer."

I was promoting other people's products through affiliate programs, and the check I got was in Canadian dollars. I was like, "I don't know. Is this real?"

I had no idea what I was doing. I was young and didn't even have a bank account. It was funny. My stepdad ended up taking me to a bank and helping me get the check cashed. He was the first person that I ever heard say "Making money while you sleep." That was the coolest thing and stuck with me.

I just ignored negative people and their advice. I ignored anything that had to do with telling me no. I was a kid who didn't listen, which turned out to be good in this case. Most people started to realize this after a while and kind of eased up, but there was always someone reminding me, "This could be a scam."

As I went through high school, opinions changed quickly because I started doing a lot of things with the marketing stuff I learned online. I liked magic and that was how I originally made money online, by promoting other people's magic tricks as an affiliate. I decided I wanted to try and be a magician myself, but after doing that for a while, I found out that I liked marketing more than I liked doing the magic.

LESSONS LEARNED

All the newsletters I signed up for would tell me that I needed to build and optimize a website then get traffic, but they didn't actually tell me how to do that.

I didn't have a whole lot of money, so I had to get creative. I found all of these different affiliate programs promising I'd make 40 to 70% of all the profits from the sales of their products, and all I had to do was sign up, and it was free.

I signed up for about 185 of them over the course of two weeks, thinking somehow that was just going to make money by signing up. After a couple of weeks, I got a little discouraged. I thought, "Well, how is this going to work? I'm not making money." It turns out people have got to go to this special link that I signed up for. I think, "Okay, cool, but how is anybody going to know to go to that website link?"

I had to figure out how to get people to these links. I didn't know how to build a website, and I didn't know how to make money with a website and I didn't have a lot of time. That's when I learned about email marketing.

I did learn enough about how to setup a website so that I could get people to give me their email. I put together a bunch of free e-Books and reports that I found and said, "Hey, if you give me your email, I'll give you all this stuff for free," and it was that easy back then. People would give me their email and I would send them ads (that I didn't even have to write) with my affiliate program links. That's how I got my first check in the mail.

When I started, I think I had 65 people on my email list. I was getting the traffic from search engines without really trying. I would send an email and make a couple of sales. Then, my list grew to 120, and I made four sales. I learned that lesson very early, as your email list grows, so does your income. A lot of people don't get that when they're starting out.

I was very cheap in the beginning because I had to be. But when I became successful I still didn't like spending money; I just got used to NOT spending money to do stuff. It was almost a cockiness.

One of the things I decided I didn't need to spend money on was insurance. I told myself, "I can afford to pay for all that stuff if anything happens or I need medication." Then one day, I had a terrible accident and literally lost everything. I didn't have health insurance or full coverage on my car. I learned my lesson from that experience.

The accident helped me to see that there was more to life than success in business. I had to be smart, wise and educated in every aspect because life can throw you a curve ball and you have to be prepared to take those punches.

Not having the insurance was a huge failure, but it was a good learning experience. I learned to listen, especially to people that are smarter and wiser than me.

Remember, I was that kid that just wouldn't listen. I've learned now to at least listen because sometimes listening is all you have to do. One of my favorite quotes is, "If a wise man listens, he'll be wiser still." No matter how smart you are, no matter how much experience you have, it's always beneficial to at least listen.

BACK TO THE START:
Advice to My Pre-Entrepreneur Self

Don't just listen to the experts. Listen to your mentors, your customers, and your students. Listening is the key to any invention.

Even though I just said you should be willing to listen, it doesn't mean you should take every piece of advice, especially the advice that you didn't ask for, advice that is freely given. Only take the advice of those who understand your passion, your drive, your motivation, and your aspiration.

Take action; you will learn more by doing than by just thinking too long about what to do next or how to do it.

Don't be afraid of failure. Realize that failure is not who you are. It's just a situation. You only fail if you quit; so there is no such thing as failure. There is only quitting.

You also can't just wait for things to happen. I had a pastor who once said, "Good things come to those who wait, but great things come to those who go get it."

Don't wait for the seeds of greatness to grow. You have to water them. You have to take action.

About Anthony Smith

Anthony Smith is a best-selling author, publisher, USA TODAY Contributor, and leading expert in local online marketing, helping business owners use the Internet to generate more leads and build a powerful online presence.

He is the "Secret Weapon" behind several digital marketing and SEO agencies where he and his team have TRIPLED and even QUADRUPLED the incomes of a substantial group of businesses over the last several years and counting.

His strategies have worked for doctors, chiropractors, lawyers, dentists, contractors, and more!

If you would like to double or triple YOUR business starting in the next 30 days using the Internet, the media, or PR then contact Anthony using the details below.

Anthony Smith Marketing

WEBSITE
AnthonyDSmith.com

EMAIL
queries@anthonydsmith.com

TWITTER
@asmithmarketing

FACEBOOK
Facebook.com/AnthonySmithMarketing

PHONE
989-941-6846

LINKEDIN
LinkedIn.com/in/AnthonySmithMarketing

DAVE McGARRY

THE START: Journey To Entrepreneurship

I don't have one of those great stories about building a baseball card trading business, or how I started up a lemonade stand that I ended up selling to a friend. But I always had an interest in making money. As a kid, I did mow lawns, and I also got involved with investing in stocks early on because my mom was a broker. I bought Disney stock. I had entrepreneurship in the DNA. I was always trying to figure out ways to use the capital I had to make more money.

In school, I was an A/B student, but I could have probably applied myself more. I focused all my time and energy on playing sports. That was probably my biggest driving factor, becoming better at sports; school was not my priority, but I did well enough to get by.

My goal was to go to the University of Florida, but I wasn't the best test taker. My SAT and ACT scores weren't that high, so I had to work harder to get in. My dad had his own landscaping business, and I worked for him over the summers mowing lawns in Florida. That's what made me stay in school to get a degree. I was the only one in my family to have done that.

CROSSING OVER:
From "I'm going to be" to "I am" an Entrepreneur

I went on to graduate school to get an MBA, and it was in an entrepreneurship class that I had one of those ah-ha moments. Our instructor was not kind. If we thought we had a great idea, he would tear us down, but it was very eye opening.

After I graduated, I became an independent contractor working for a guy who had a fitness studio. I got to see a little bit more about how the ownership side of the business worked. He was obviously making more than I was getting paid for doing the same thing.

One of my multimillionaire clients gave me the book "Rich Dad, Poor Dad" by Robert Kiyosaki. That book as well as "Cash Flow Quadrant" which talks about being an employee, a self-employed business owner, and an investor, definitely inspired me.

I always wanted more. I was never content. That was an internal struggle for me, but a good thing. I was always trying to find out how I could do more, how I could become more.

During the recession, the club I was working for developed financial problems and had to lay off the entire management staff. I was stuck at a crossroad and had to ask myself, "Ok, what do I do? Should I try to find another job or do I go out on my own and start something?" After talking with my wife, we decided that it was the time to do it. That is when I started my first online business.

Most of my family were business owners, and they have always been supportive of me. My father-in-law was a business owner as well and was very supportive, too. I have friends who are not entrepreneurs, but they have that business, entrepreneurial spirit and are very supportive. I have never had any issues about that. It has been a blessing.

LESSONS LEARNED

I decided that I was not going to start my own gym because of the overhead and some of the stuff that I had seen with the financials. So,

I started my first online business called Workingmomworkouts.com. It was an online membership site that provided fitness workouts for working moms.

One thing I did was join a networking group which allowed me to expand my sphere of influence with other business owners. It provided me with an opportunity get out there and start seeing what other business owners were struggling with and getting some help with my issues as well.

This was also an opportunity to discover more about myself, who I really am, because once you get thrown into the entrepreneurship pool, you are the boss. There's nobody saying, "Hey, I need this thing done." You have to put those deadlines on yourself.

Mindset was a huge factor. There are lots of highs and lows with entrepreneurship. Seth Godin has a book called "The Dip." It's basically about the highs and lows. You set out and, man, everything's great. You're doing all this stuff and getting results, and then all of a sudden something happens and, bam, there's nothing coming in, and you're like, "Okay, what happened? What am I going to do?"

Most entrepreneurs I know have ups and downs. My first experience with this made me question if I was in the right niche and if I needed to change. I definitely had some dips in that area.

I ended up working with a business coach. Even though I had an MBA, I felt like I still needed somebody to hold me accountable and help me. This guy was really good. One of the things that I did not have as one of my line items was a direct payment to myself. I had all my expenses down, but there was no line item for payment to me.

I found out a lot of small business owners only pay themselves when and if there is money left over. That was me. My business coach explained that when you do your profit/loss statement, there had better be a line item where you put down a fixed salary for yourself. You are getting paid a certain amount and even if you are losing money, you still need to be paid. That was a big lesson for me.

Don't be stubborn and unwilling to change. That was a valuable lesson. At some point, you have to pivot and evolve. I think a lot of entrepreneurs take the stand, "Man, I don't care, its hell or high water and I am going to do this." They know that the market has changed, but they refuse to change with it. These are things that I learned from that first venture, and they continue to help me now here in the present.

I can't do it all. Sometimes as a small business owner, you try to do everything. I have to delegate and outsource because that frees me up to do the things that I am passionate about doing. When I do that, I have much more energy, and I feel great about it. When I start doing other tasks that I know I am not good at like spending hours trying to use Photoshop to do graphic design and then seeing how awful it turns out, brings me down. I realized that I have got to do the things that I am best at, and outsource or delegate those things that I'm not good at doing.

Being an entrepreneur is much different than being an employee of a company. Decide if you need to have the stability of a steady, fixed paycheck. If so, then being an entrepreneur is not going to be easy for you because there are so many highs, lows, and changes.

It takes self-introspection. Do you have the ability to face adversity and tackle adversity when times get tough? To know whether or not you're able to hang on and not give up, because there's going to be times where you're going to want to quit.

You almost have to throw yourself out there to find out. If you go back and look at what happened with people like Steve Jobs or Mark

Cuban, they had the mindset that no matter what, they would fail and fail and fail, until they succeeded. They just never quit.

About Dave McGarry

Dave currently provides online fitness coaching for those who are 40 and over. His online fitness training doesn't just focus on weight loss but creating the mindset, habits, and beliefs that allow someone to achieve their goals as well. His program helps people realize what is preventing them from achieving their goals, and then he coaches them to push past those limiting beliefs and reach greater success.

Dave takes off his fitness coach hat and puts on his Dad hat to coach his two daughters' soccer teams. He finds being there for his daughters every step of the way is very important to him. Keeping himself in shape is also a high priority for him.

McGarry Wellness Solutions

WEBSITE
FitOver40Challenge.com

FACEBOOK
Facebook.com/DaveMcGarry

EMAIL
dave@davemcgarry.com

TWITTER
@davemcgarry

LINKEDIN
LinkedIn.com/in/DavidMcGarry

INSTAGRAM
davidsmcgarry

JESS AND SARA OWEN

THE START: Journey To Entrepreneurship

Jess Owen: My family owns a resort on the Washington coast, and I grew up in the business. I worked jobs in housekeeping, maintenance, the front desk, night audit, dishwasher, busboy, server, host, bartender, and executive chef. I thought that owning and running a business is how you do things.

I wasn't a very good student. Mainly because it was too easy for me, I could ace tests, so I didn't like going through the mechanics of doing the daily homework and all that other mumbo jumbo.

When I was a teenager, my friends and I ran our espresso cart in front of the resort before the restaurant opened. I always liked the idea of being able to do my own thing and generate income; to be the master of my own destiny. I never really thought about career options growing up, I just wanted to run the family business.

It was while I was building a website for the resort that I started learning about the Internet and search engine optimization. When I was able to get the resort's website ranked on the first page of Google, it made me think that this was a skill that I could market and other businesses would find helpful.

Sara Owen: I grew up completely different. Both of my parents were cops. However, I started training horses at a very early age. When I was 11, I was giving riding lessons and showing horses professionally. Without realizing it, it was my own little business.

I had to work a lot harder in school than Jess; it didn't come easy for me. I was an average student with B's and C's. I loved History, English, Literature, and anything where I could debate or read.

As a teenager, when I wasn't giving riding lessons or going to school, I would work in the tack and feed store my parents opened. In the summer I also worked various jobs at a burger stand, restaurants, hotel front desk, and some retail. That was horrible.

I would say I more or less fell into being an entrepreneur when I met Jess. I was 19 and trying to figure out what I wanted to be when I grew up, and Jess was 21. I had never met somebody that young, who had known pretty much all of his life what he wanted to do. He wanted to run his family's business and carry on their legacy. So after we got married, we moved to work at the resort.

My inspiration for becoming an entrepreneur was when our oldest son got to his junior year of high school and started talking about going to culinary school. Then our youngest began talking about Harvard. I thought, "We need to make some extra money."

I was already doing social media and website marketing for the resort, and I wouldn't call it an epiphany—but I just thought about how I could help the other business owners in my community do the same… while making some extra money to put my kids through college.

CROSSING OVER:
From "I'm going to be" to "I am" an Entrepreneur

Sara Owen: Jess was building websites, and I was doing social media marketing with Facebook, Twitter, and YouTube. I would call on his expertise, or he would call on mine. We had businesses that wanted to hire both of us to help them with this stuff. We were working with each other so often we decided to become Owen Marketing Group.

Jess Owen: The county surrounding the resort and where we live is made up of very small communities totaling about 7000 people. Everybody knows everybody. The business culture out here has always been that businesses help each other. We're competing with restaurants down the street, but if they run out of romaine lettuce, they'll give us a call, we'll lend them some until the next delivery comes in, and then they pay it back, that's how we've always done it.

When we developed these online marketing skills, and we saw other people struggling, we thought, "Well shoot; we can help them out and help build up the entire area."

The experience of discovering that I had another marketable skill outside of what I grew up with and had always been doing was a new realization for me, and it was very exciting to be able to go out and talk to other businesses and help them in the community.

At the same time, it's like an actor being typecast because the community knows me for being a chef at the resort. My family even thought, "Why would he want to do anything else"? It was hard to get people to view me as a digital marketing and social media expert as well.

Sara Owen: After about 15 years, it felt exhilarating to step out and do something else. You get used to what you do. While I was not necessarily in a rut, I knew with my training and knowledge I could help others.

Like Jess, people associated me with the resort. I had to convince them that I was knowledgeable about other things as well. When I first started, they thought Facebook was a fad, and it was hard to get them to take it seriously. I had to stress, "Yes, you absolutely do need a website; you do need to be part of the conversation." It is something we tell business owners all the time, whether we were teaching a class or doing a presentation for the Chamber of Commerce, or doing a one-on-one, "People are talking about you online."

My family was incredibly supportive. On the other hand, our friends thought we were nuts because when you work for family and your family owns a resort, you already work 60, 70 hours a week.

Because we do still work for our family's resort, we only have room for so many clients and those spots are filled with very happy clients. We currently run all of the marketing for a chocolate festival, which is a blast. Not only do we get to create all of their marketing, but also there's always chocolate involved.

We do have people who are waiting to become clients, but I would have to say that with our limited capacity, we're very happy with how things are going. We love to work together, and we work together well. It's a lot of fun, and honestly, Jess and I pretty much have fun no matter what we do.

LESSONS LEARNED

Jess Owen: If had it to do over, I would be more cautious about giving or discounting away services too much to get my foot in the door. Doing free work was a mistake because they will not value what you've done for them in the end.

In the restaurant, we always knew that the people who spent the most money were always the happiest customers we had. It seems like it is true in the Owen Marketing Group as well. The people that are spending the money are always pleased with the results. The people that got a freebie, along with stellar results, don't care that much because they were not part of it, they didn't have anything invested in it.

Sara Owen: When I first started, I thought, "I can do Facebook, after all, I talk to my brother on Facebook." I was so used to writing ad copy that when I began writing social media content, it was all calls to action and urgency. When writing a magazine or a radio ad, you only get that one opportunity to get your point across. But social media is so much warmer than magazine or radio ads; it's about building a relationship. I had to learn to build a relationship and have a conversation with the customer instead of trying to sell all the time.

That was a big realization, and I likened it to when I was a kid; I would go to the hardware store with my dad. The employees at the hardware store knew him; they asked him what he was working on, and they had a relationship. You can do that through social media marketing, and I love that.

I used to love working in the dining room with Jess and getting to know our guests in the hotel. Those people kept coming back, and I developed relationships with them. When I first started doing social media marketing, I was getting in my own way, but now I feel like I'm really good at developing relationships.

BACK TO THE START:
Advice to My Pre-Entrepreneur Self

Jess Owen: It doesn't have to be perfect. It just has to be good.

Sara Owen: My advice would be, go for it, don't be afraid, and be patient. It will happen, you will get there and your hard work will pay off.

About Jess and Sara Owen

With Jess growing up in the entrepreneurial lifestyle and Sara coming into it, it allows them to have two different perspectives on marketing and selling their services to other business. They currently run Owen Marketing Group, which helps restaurants, hospitality, and resorts market and run their websites properly. Jess and Sara are also the sole marketers for a chocolate festival.

Sara loves cooking Jess Southern meals, and Jess loves eating them even more. They enjoy breaking away from their business and vacationing in Mexico for a week every year. One of the hardest challenges they have for their home life is trying to have a sit-down family dinner every Sunday.

Owen Marketing GROUP

WEBSITE
OwenMarketingGroup.com

FACEBOOK
Facebook.com/OMGOceanShores

PHONE
541-622-2989

EMAIL
OMG@OwenMarketingGROUP.com

DORINA LANZA

THE START: Journey To Entrepreneurship

I was always an overachiever. I left high school at sixteen. They gave me the diploma at seventeen. I finished college at eighteen, majoring in math. I was always thinking, "If you cannot do something and be in the top one percent, you should not do it at all." I also discovered that it's not an endearing trait when I would say those kinds of things. It is better to shut up and do instead of pontificating about it.

I was also very unsure of myself. Always feeling fat, dumb and ugly. What I saw in the mirror was not congruent with what I believed. What I believed about myself was that I was not good enough, nobody liked me, and I would never fit in because there must be something wrong with me. When I look back at pictures of myself, I wonder what the hell was I thinking?

I didn't have any trouble in the sciences. I have most of a Ph.D. in math and wound up starting out as a medical physicist and then an aeronautical engineer.

I was on the faculty of Northeastern University for twenty years. The students either loved me or hated me, most of them loved me, and they did very well.

I discovered I had a knack for alienating people in corporations. I never really fit in. When I got my MBA and went into management consulting, for some reason my colleagues didn't seem to relate well to me.

My entry to entrepreneurship was forced on me when I left that company. I had no choice. I realized that I wasn't cut out to be in a corporate hierarchy. Even though I didn't fit in with my colleagues, the clients liked me. That's when I became an independent management consultant. I would strategize with my clients and help them figure out how to grow their businesses.

CROSSING OVER:
From "I'm going to be" to "I am" an Entrepreneur

Growing up, I was involved in activities around my community like sailing and skiing. This is where I met some very successful entrepreneurs. I didn't realize until later in life that they didn't just fall from the sky into their positions. They actually built something.

One day I got a phone call from a sailing friend's mother who told me about this guy who had a Ph.D. in chemistry and started working in a network marketing business. Now he had built an organization that was paying him fifty thousand dollars a month. I thought, "Geez if he can do it, I can certainly do it." So I signed up, and I went to work. It was the blind following the blind, but I wound up building a big organization and a nice stream of income.

I was an entrepreneur before I recognized that I was an entrepreneur. Getting to the top of four different network marketing companies taught me that in order to attract business, you need to become an attractor of people. It was my success with network marketing that made me realize that I was an attractor of people and that I could teach others how to become an attractor of people as well.

I created a system that taught people how to become the attractors they needed to be to build their own business. When I was finally able to articulate this, it hit me over the head, "Oh yeah, wow, yeah, I'm an entrepreneur!"

I got the classic response that most people get, "Why don't you go out and get a good job?" My people are not entrepreneurs. Most people need to have a sure thing. If they don't have a salary, they don't know what to do, and they are very risk averse. Of course, my siblings, they didn't care. My father was the opposite of encouraging.

I didn't get any grief from friends at all. Most of the people I hung around had that entrepreneur gene anyway. The majority of my friends are not employee types. Most of them have accomplished something that took self-determination to get there.

The ultimate validation is when you get your check.

LESSONS LEARNED

I realized two things, that I am terrible at starting people from ground zero because I do not have the patience.

When I was a ski instructor, they learned never to give me the beginners. When I was a math professor, they knew never to assign me the students that needed remedial algebra. Everything I have done teaching, I have learned that I shine in the top tier. I do not go after people who are just starting their business. I do not want to be in the market teaching "Beginning Sales 101" or "How to Get Your First Ten Clients."

I also learned that I have to be good at managing cash flow because there are gaps when money isn't coming in. I've seen many entrepreneurs make the mistake of mortgaging themselves to the hilt because they assumed that whatever high income they were getting at some time was going to continue. But when they hit a gap, all of the sudden they're bankrupt.

BACK TO THE START:
Advice to My Pre-Entrepreneur Self

Start on your personal development journey as soon as possible. Don't wait until you are in your forties.

Find somebody to work with who can teach you what they have learned in such a way that you can internalize it and live it. That will accelerate your success. I had to figure out everything by myself. Occasionally, I would pick up something from somebody. But I look back and realize that I would have done much better with a mentor.

About Dorina Lanza

Dorina Lanza excels in every activity. She puts in 110% into everything she does. She graduated from college at the very young age of 18 with a major in Math, received her Master's in Math at age 20, and then went back to get her MBA in Strategic Planning and International Business. She is one of the few who truly loves what she does. To her, work does not even feel like work. She escapes the long workweeks by skiing and relaxing by the beach. She also enjoys her new house with her husband and living each day to the fullest.

Dorina is co-founder and CEO of LIMB Software Systems, LLC and is on the board of trustees for Nashua Humane Society. She has recently updated her 8-week program where she teaches people how the brain works, how you attract people, why they come to you and how to leverage that yourself.

White Tiger Group, LLC

WEBSITE
DorinaLanza.com

FACEBOOK
Facebook.com/DorinaLanza

LINKEDIN
LinkedIn.com/in/DorinaLanza

TWITTER
@dorinalanza

JACK AUSTIN

THE START: Journey To Entrepreneurship

A lot of people talk about how young they were when they started businesses. I tried to start by mowing lawns when I was nine, but my over-protective dad wouldn't let me. That shut me down until my teens when I began doing weed clearing and grove work in the agricultural community where we lived.

I wasn't a good student, even though I was a bit bookish and very solitary. In third grade I had a teacher, who was retiring, that told the class that she didn't understand why everybody had to learn the multiplication tables because it didn't make any sense to her for all the time spent on rote memorization rather than something more useful. So I took her at her word and didn't bother to memorize them. This caused me to get labeled as somebody who "could not learn." I was considered borderline learning disabled and in the fourth grade, I was put into a Special Ed class located in a trailer in front of the Mae Ellis Elementary School. I found this stigmatizing.

And still there was a Silver Lining. It was in that fourth grade Special Ed class that I learned how to touch type and read at a college level. I was out of the class in half of a year.

After very mixed experiences in multiple school systems, I ended up becoming the school photographer my Sophomore year of high school. I shot more than ninety percent of the photographs for the yearbook and did an internship with the Orange County Register (a regional daily newspaper competing with the Los Angeles Times).

This internship gave me the opportunity to meet with people who were working with National Geographic and other major publications.

After high school, I stopped being a photographer because I wanted to be acknowledged as myself, not the function I fulfilled at school. I was accepted at Trinity University, a private liberal arts college in San Antonio, Texas, where I got a degree in Philosophy with minors in Journalism and Psychology. Trinity was a real self-mastery experience due to my educational past.

There was a long period where I waited tables and under-performed. I was living in San Antonio, going to school. I met my ex-wife and spent the next twenty years living in Texas.

Suddenly, at the age of thirty, I developed an internal awareness that I needed to have a more stable career-oriented job, more security and something that allowed me more respect from my family. It was like an internal clock was ticking. I ended up getting a corporate management job working for Red Lobster, then a Division of Darden Restaurants, Inc.

I was slowed in my career advancement because my wife and I had lived in Austin since 1984 and didn't want to leave, but as soon as my ex-wife and I separated, my boss asked, "Would you take the promotion to Killeen?" I said, "Yes." He said, "Are you sure?"

Killeen is a town right outside the largest army base in the world. It was a mess; the restaurant took three part-time general managers to try and hold it together. I said yes and spent nine years as a general manager.

Then stuff hit the fan. I was freshly divorced, had filed bankruptcy, and had been kicked to the curb by a rebound relationship. My unresolved personal issues, drinking too much, and all the stuff that I had not addressed after the divorce came crashing down on me. It was at this point I discovered Tony Robbins' work. It was the thing that allowed me to shift the way I looked at my world and to become the leader I needed to be. That brought me to domination. I learned that there was a set of tools about stepping up in the world and coming forward in a dynamic way that allowed other people to say, "Yes. I am willing to take the risk too."

The turnover rate at the restaurant, meaning the rate at which staff turned over, was 300%. The division goal was 167%. In six months we had it reduced to 54%. I held it there for two years – an unheard standard in the industry. We had become a premier employer.

People began taking ownership for their jobs. They did so because I learned how to connect and communicate with them in a way where we could establish a structure that made a difference. This is when my entrepreneurial bug caught on because I realized that I could make a bigger impact with people. Literally, divorces were avoided because of the changes people were having in their work environment. Their self-esteem rose causing them to take different actions with their spouses, therefore producing better marriages.

CROSSING OVER:
From "I'm going to be" to "I am" an Entrepreneur

After sixteen years in the business, I realized I had to go out on my own.

The moment I thought I had it all together, my mom was diagnosed with cancer. Since I was not working sixty plus hours a week, I had the time to connect with her before she passed away. There was a self-image thing going on for me at the same time and moving through the work that I had to do to be able to surface it; I became aware of how to address it. It was a painful blessing in disguise.

My friends and family kind of ignored what I was doing. That has to do with how I was perceived. Gay Hendricks points out in the book, The Big Leap, that when he made his big leap into full self-expression he discovered that there was something that had always been holding him back. Now this guy has a Ph.D. from Stanford. His relationships are not working out the way that he wants them to. He does not have the money that he wants and so on. This situation was almost identical to mine. It is called an upper limit barrier. It is an unconscious thing. Everybody has some version of it, but nobody understands it until they try to push the envelope.

Start changing an identity and a lot of people may get push back from family and friends, but there is an internal push back. Bubbles you have to pop to be able to have it work because otherwise people will push against it, again and again. They find themselves back where they were, like a rubber band that pulls them to a position. The discovery that I made was that when I went independent, the things I got were like a cosmic reward.

I ended up learning how to invest in real estate, which did not pan out because I did not have the skill set of closing which comes down to being able to sit in pain with a client. Not to take on their pain, but be there with them while they realize that there is something they have been avoiding and need to address. I have found that this is true in sales of all degrees. It is phenomenal how much avoidance people develop before they come to the realization they have got to do something. Denial is a powerful status quo mechanism.

There is the intention: "I am going to help this person whether they like it or not. I am going to be close enough to them and be trustworthy enough that they can feel that it is okay. It is trust and respect."

I have got to hold the negative space for them long enough for them to feel it so that they realize they do not want this pain. They have to do something about it. If I do not do something, if I do not do this "space holding", they will go through absolute hell. It could take them years to get over it unless I take responsibility to connect with them at a deep enough level and hold the space while they decide. I only fully learned that skill of holding that space in my consulting and coaching business because it is the same thing. People fear powerful transformation, even when they desire it.

LESSONS LEARNED

It is an intimate experience because you are talking about changing some of the most delicate places in a person's life. People want it, but they fear it at the same time. They do not realize what it is going to take and their unconscious ego mind is saying, "Run away, run away, run away."

It is not going to get better on it's own. You are going to do the same thing over and over again in different patterns until you own the fact that you have to take just a little bit of pain, walk through resistance, so you do not lay on your death bed with regret.

People have to come to that decision point themselves because if I say it, it is a lie. Their ego will tell them it is a lie. When they say it, it is the truth.

There is a turning point inside when a person realizes that you are not there to get something from them. You are there to serve and give something to them. They have to surrender internally "It is going to be okay" or the pain is going to get worse. When people are in denial they will do everything to avoid it. They run around busily trying to medicate it in various ways: by busyness, avoidance, prescription or illicit drugs, porn, sex, work. None of these vehicles will take them through the barrier. They distract. They only dull the pain for a while.

I learned a lesson about putting my toe in instead of being fully committed. There is chicken interest, and there is pig commitment.

When you talk about bacon and eggs breakfast, a chicken has a limited commitment. It lays some eggs, and they are on the plate, but the pig went all the way.

The limiting belief that people did not like me; I developed that belief early in grade school, and it was a made up story that held me back. The gap was closed when I learned how the only truth was in my ego's involvement. In other words, my ego needed to be right so it would show me every time that somebody did not respond the way I wanted them to or did not automatically fully accept me. It was pushing through the discomfort of getting truly close to people and let them trust me by showing how much I care, so they could take a risk and trust themselves.

People have a lot of that experience in their life where over and over they do not complete. They fall short, stop trying, give up, half commit, and they start losing faith in themselves. They are out of integrity and lose credibility with themselves.

I learned that it was not about me being a superman. It was about me learning that we all shared these same characteristics, as long as I was not trying to be safe by keeping distance. I did not have to look smarter or prove myself. The more I became present with people and stayed through the initial discomfort of gaining trust; the more everybody got what they wanted. People had breakthroughs, and I consistently relived that breakthrough of having let down my guard, dropping the invulnerable persona.

BACK TO THE START:
Advice to My Pre-Entrepreneur Self

In the late 70s, Arnold Schwarzenegger made a movie when he was focused on bodybuilding called Stay Hungry. It was an indie film. I think it's an entrepreneurial message. Stay Hungry because that is what keeps a person right at their growth edge.

About Jack Austin

Jack Austin has been providing life guidance to others for over 30 years. He grew up experiencing many hardships and did not realize his calling until midlife. Now he helps others break through the invisible barriers that are holding them, their careers, and businesses back.

Each client brings unique, individual challenges to Jack and he uses the strength and insight gained from his personal struggles that he pushed through, as well as cutting-edge technologies and expertise, to lead them. In all this, he shows how compassionate he is about his work and what he is willing to do to help his clients, always putting them first.

Jack Austin is the CEO of Quantum Breakthroughs. He consults CEOs, executives, business owners and entrepreneurs in advancing their business by assisting them through the invisible walls. He teaches them to be ethical and create a business founded on servant leadership, cultural engagement, and social responsibility. Jack emphasizes that just because a certain method of command and control leadership has worked in the past does not mean that it will work under the current social and cultural conditions.

Even with his hectic schedule, Jack makes sure to take some time to himself and rejuvenate. On the weekends he can be found hiking, climbing, or mountain biking. Physical activity is a must for him, getting at least 15 minutes of cardio a day and going to the gym every chance he gets.

Jack Austin

WEBSITE
JackAustin.com

FACEBOOK
Facebook.com/JackLAustin

EMAIL
jack@jackaustin.com

PHONE
949-200-0116

LINKEDIN
LinkedIn.com/in/JackAustinQuantumBreakthroughs

JIMENA CORTES

THE START: Journey To Entrepreneurship

When I was a kid, I would watch movies that had scenes with people in big conference rooms, and I always thought that would be me. From very early on, I wanted that kind of life.

I was always somebody who would go after what they wanted. When I was a sophomore in high school, I thought that it would be kind of cool to do a student exchange. The idea of going and living in Europe was very appealing to me. I asked myself, "If that is what I want to do, what steps do I need to take to make it happen?" I did the research. I filled out the applications. I got the money, and I went. I always knew if I wanted something, then there is a way to get it; I only need to figure it out.

I grew up very poor. I was born in Costa Rica, and we moved to the United States when my mother got married. She always worked in the restaurant business and dreamed of having her own. I would get frustrated with her and ask, "Why don't you start your own restaurant?" It seemed so simple to me.

I knew if I wanted to be wealthy and have that kind of lifestyle, I would need to be the head of my empire. I decided that I was not going to talk about wanting things; I was going to get them. Somebody out there is getting it, so why can't it be me? That was my mindset.

CROSSING OVER:
From "I'm going to be" to "I am" an Entrepreneur

I started my first business when I was eighteen. I had a friend who was working in the travel business, and he told me, "Look, this is what I do. This is how I do it." I thought, "Really? I could do that." We decided to go into business together because we had different strengths and thought that would make us good business partners. In other words, I took the first opportunity that came along. It was good for a while. It was also a big learning experience.

I have always been lucky to have very encouraging people around me. They understand the way I am and know that when I want something, I go get it. My mom was always very encouraging, and people are always challenging me, "Yeah, if that is what you want to do, go see what happens."

When I started my SEO company, the first six months were terrible. I only had one client, and I tried everything from business networking events to Craigslist. I was not having much success, so I started to look for a job again. I was using LinkedIn for my job search, and I noticed that the target audiences that I wanted to have as clients were there.

I started networking on LinkedIn and within two weeks I got my second client. I was excited and thought, "Wow, there is something to this." I kept networking on LinkedIn, and that's how I was able to grow my business to six figures. Today my company still has the SEO side of things, but I also have a LinkedIn 'Done For You' service and a LinkedIn training course that teaches others how to use LinkedIn as an effective lead generation tool.

LESSONS LEARNED

I learned a few things in that business. The first was to be more careful about the people that you work with, especially if they are your business partner because it's like a marriage. Sometimes it's even more complicated than a marriage because you are working together and spending more time together than with anyone else.

My partner started to spend money on things that were not business related and that we should not be doing. I told him that I thought we should reinvest in the business and grow it, not buy expensive televisions. Since he was much older than me, I had decided to go into business with him because I thought he would be able to lead me. What ended up happening was that I was leading him!

I ended up leaving the business. I was only nineteen and a half years old. I didn't have the money to start a new business and had to go work for someone else. That was painful, and I was not able to start my next business until I was twenty-five.

That horrible experience has taught me to choose partners a little bit better. I know now that I have to be more careful when I decide to work with someone. I make sure that they really do have strengths and weaknesses that complement mine, and that they are good people.

One of the things that happened to me, and this is very eye-opening, was I had an employee that I had to let go. He was getting ready to start his own business and was taking everything I taught him and was going to become my competition. When I found this out, I told him, "You know what? You don't need to work here another month. You are done."

When I did that, he emailed all my clients to badmouth me. Then he offered them the same services at half the price.

The lesson I learned there was to get better paperwork in place so people are scared to do that because they cannot legally contact your clients afterward.

I also learned not to give anybody too much information. The way I run my business now is on every client campaign, one person does one part of it, and another person does the other part of it. That way one person doesn't know the entire strategy and can't go off and do it themselves. It's helped me avoid that happening again.

BACK TO THE START:
Advice to My Pre-Entrepreneur Self

Look at your finances closely. My first year in business, I made sixty-five thousand dollars, but I didn't know where it went. I was working a lot, but I was not making any money.

I discovered that I was not paying attention to my expenses. I was taking on work and not charging appropriately, and I was spending too much to get certain things done. When I realized this, I started to look closely at my profit and loss statement. Now, I take about an hour every Saturday, and look at all the credit card statements, making sure that I am not being overcharged for anything because that happens a lot.

Being an entrepreneur, it's not easy, and it's not for everyone. There are few, if any, four-hour workweeks. I think about my business twenty-four/seven. It's a lot more work and more challenging than a 9-5 job, but I wouldn't trade it for anything. To make more money than most people ever make at my age and to have the freedom to travel, makes it worth the journey.

About Jimena Cortes

Starting at a young age, Jimena Cortes knew she was born to be an entrepreneur. Her first business partnership began when she was only 18 years old! Running her businesses was not easy, and she faced a few trial and errors. Even though many of her initial businesses ended in failure, she was not slowed down from her path of becoming a successful entrepreneur. Today she owns a highly successful marketing agency and has taught over 4,000 professionals worldwide how to use LinkedIn to get clients.

Jimena enjoys the freedom her business gives her to travel the world (because she can work from anywhere as long as she has an Internet connection) while making an impact in the world through helping her clients' and students' businesses flourish.

Wizard Media LLC

WEBSITE
WizardMedia.net

FACEBOOK
Facebook.com/Jimenaytb

EMAIL
info@wizardmedia.net

PHONE
702-285-5664

LINKEDIN
LinkedIn.com/in/JimenaCortes

ARMAND AGUILLON

THE START: Journey To Entrepreneurship

I always wanted to be in business. When I was eight years old, I would go to neighbors' houses and ask, "Can I wash your car?" I'd get like $.50 or $1. The moment I got pushed into it as when I was a teenager. My goals were wishy-washy until I saw one of my mom's superannuation statements (similar to a 401K statement). I knew it was not going to be enough for her to live on and it drove me and my goals changed because of it. I thought, "Now, I've got to be able to help provide for my mom and my family, I've got to save some money to buy a house," which we ended up doing.

The first proper job I had was working in a pet shop that belonged to a friend of my mom's. I also worked in retail and entertainment, from Sea World to casinos, and then worked my way up from there before starting my own business.

My mom gave me this book and said, "Go ahead and read this." It just sat there on my shelf for three or four years before I picked it up to read. It was "Cash-Flow Quadrant" by Robert Kiyosaki. I read the book and thought, "Wow. This is awesome!" From that, I discovered "Rich Dad, Poor Dad," which got me reading more and gave me a more focused intent on business.

CROSSING OVER:
From "I'm going to be" to "I am" an Entrepreneur

After reading "Rich Dad, Poor Dad" and "Cash-Flow Quadrant," we organized a Cash-Flow game in the Gold Coast. It just so happened that a couple of Kiyosaki's best friends were coming over to visit their daughter, who was attending school. They found out about our Cash-Flow Club games and contacted us and said, "Hey, I'll come over and teach you guys!" They taught us how to play the game the way the rich played it. It was even more eye opening than reading the books. From that club, I met a lot of people. One of them happened to be my current business partner.

My biggest support was from my family, my mom, and my sisters. But there were other people close to me saying, "You can't do that. Why don't you just quit and get a job? You're not going to make it." That drove me even more because I wanted to prove them wrong!

I started out promoting a big Health Expo, which is ironic because I was spending so much time working on it that I wasn't taking care of my health properly. As we got closer to the event, things became very, very hard. Finances were strained. The money would come in and then it would go right back out. It was like we had a hole in our pocket. There were times I would just want to pull out and think, "Oh, no. I can't do it," and my business partner would say, "No, no, no. We have got to do this." I'm glad I had my business partner with me. We would be there to support each other because sometimes he would be the doubtful one and I would say, "We can't pull out now. We can do this!"

Even though I set my own hours, it was really time consuming. This was back in the dial-up Internet days when you got data speeds of two kilobytes per second. I remember how we would be ready to send an email and all of a sudden a fax would come in, and it would cut off because we were only running on one phone line.

Since it was dial-up, it could get bogged down and cut off so I would wake up at 2:00 or 3:00 in the morning to make sure it was running. If I saw it was in standby mode, I knew it was down and think, "Oh, no. I've got to get it running again."

It seemed like we never slept for nine months in preparation for this 3-day event. Then people loved us when we had the event going. We knew everyone by name and what they were doing. I almost felt that I knew their families even though I had only ever spoken to them on the phone. Then they would come to the event, and his helped us put a face to the name.

It was very challenging but positive. I think I learned more about myself than about the business. Even though we were only hitting the break-even point, it was more money than I was earning previously.

LESSONS LEARNED

I learned that you have to develop tenacity when you are in business. You can't just be too nice to everyone. I'm not saying that you have to be arrogant, but you have to be firm.

As a first-time business owner, it is hard to position yourself as an expert in the field. Businesses would ask us, "Who are you guys?" Then would say, "We've never heard of you. We want to go with someone established who has done this before," and then they would hang up. We had a lot of those types of calls. Finally, I sat down with my business partner and said, "How are we going to fix this?"

We brainstormed and started thinking, "What's in it for them?" Always, always asking, "What's in it for them? Why would they want to do business with us?" We wrote down a whole list. What's in it for the visitors? I came up with an idea of how we could approach the local council. Here in Australia, a Council is the equivalent of a County in America.

We were able to set up a meeting with a woman from the Council. When we sat down, she said, "Okay, you guys have five minutes. What do you want?" It was straightforward and we needed to be upfront. We told her that we were organizing a big expo to be held in the area. We explained that it was a health expo and listed all the positive benefits. We concluded by asking for her endorsement and recommendation. Specifically, we were looking for a letter from her telling about the expo, encouraging people to check it out and saying she recommended us. We were delighted that we received a short letter from her with the actual council logo!

From then on, we put their logo in front of our proposals (kind of like a sponsor) so potential customers would see it and decide, "Oh, it is okay." After seeing it, the next time we contacted them, we would confirm that we have done this, and we have done that. When we then sent the proposals, they responded with, "We've heard about you guys." We had not even done anything for them yet, and they had already heard about us!

BACK TO THE START:
Advice to My Pre-Entrepreneur Self

If you want it, you should go for it, even though you are scared. At one point I was scared and thought, "Should I do this or not?" Just do it because you will learn along the way. Action will teach you preparation. You will find as you get closer to your goals you will be faced with more and more obstacles and it's going to be more and more challenging. You have to keep at it because once you finish, you will feel the greatest satisfaction.

About Armand Aguillon

Armand Aguillon runs a real estate business in Australia and has been an entrepreneur ever since he was eight years old when he ran a car wash business. He began by going door-to-door and persuading people to allow him to wash their cars. After witnessing the financial crisis his family was going through, he knew it was up to him to support his mom and sisters. He was able to secure a roof over their heads while being new to the business in a tough market. After lots of hard work, countless hours of missed sleep, and guidance, his dedication paid off. He became a successful entrepreneur.

Now he is a very successful real estate agent spending his free time with his wife, 4-year old son, and 16-year-old stepdaughter, He also enjoys golfing and practicing martial arts. He is a second-degree black belt and has been practicing for 24 years. He explains that Martial Arts is his mental getaway, allowing him to focus and recharge for the work week.

Armand Aguillon

EMAIL
wiseinvest@gmail.com

TWITTER
@ArmandAguillon

LINKEDIN
au.LinkedIn.com/in/ArmandAguillon

INSTAGRAM
armand.aguillon

FACEBOOK
Facebook.com/Armand.Aguillon

PHONE
678-667-3610

PATRICK MEJIA

THE START: Journey To Entrepreneurship

The first sign that my entrepreneurial gene kicked in was when I was ten years old. I started a bimonthly car-washing program for my neighborhood. I would knock on doors and ask if they wanted their car hand washed for a couple of dollars. It was a hit or miss business, but it was fun.

I was a C student; I didn't like Math and English. Geography and History were my favorites because my parents flew for American Airlines, so we got to travel all over the world and see different cultures. The travel bug bit me, and I wanted that lifestyle. I wanted to be independent and learn different cultures and history. I love history; I would read up on every place we went.

There was a defining moment when I was still in grammar school. I had detention after class, and I had to empty the garbage cans from the classrooms. When I was throwing the trash in the dumpster, I noticed some Easter and Christmas stamp books. They were fundraisers; you would buy ten stamps for a dollar to paste them into the books, and that money would go to charity.

I jumped in the dumpster and grabbed the books, took them home and cleaned them up. For the next two weeks, I sold the Christmas stamp books in the parking lot after church. Before I knew it, I had made $77.

I was faced with a dilemma, "Okay, what do I do with this money? Do I keep it? Do I go 50/50?" After sleeping on it I knew what I should do.

Monday morning, I took the money to the principal's office and said, "Hey, this is your money, here is how I came up with it. You guys threw out all these books, so I decided to sell them." The principal exclaimed, "Oh my God, thank you so much."

For the next two years, I was asked to train other students how to sell stamp books as well. That was the first job that I enjoyed, and I got something back from helping out.

I read "Think and Grow Rich" by Napoleon Hill and "How to Win Friends and Influence People" by Dale Carnegie when I was a kid. Those books along with a set of tapes by Tony Robins called "Personal Power", really sharpened my people skills.

CROSSING OVER:
From "I'm going to be" to "I am" an Entrepreneur

When I turned sixteen, I got a job at the grocery store as a box boy after school. This fired up my entrepreneurial appetite. I eventually worked my way up to produce night manager.

That job enabled me to buy my first car. When I went to the dealership, they were trying to upsell me an alarm system, extended warranty, and paint sealant. I kept saying, "No, no, it is too expensive." After buying my new car, I thought back to my neighborhood car washing business and just for fun; I decided to do some research and find out where I could get paint sealant.

I knew that the waxing thing was a pain in the butt. I started contacting body shops and asked, "Do you sell paint sealant? Can you help me find a place where I can find it?" I talked with a nice guy at one of the shops who gave me the name of a paint sealant wholesaler. I contacted them and bought a ton of sealant for my car. It was only $64. The dealership was going to charge me $700. I started putting it on my parents' car, my girlfriend's car and the cars of all my friends. Everybody was happy, and it kept the paint looking nice.

I figured out that a lot of people didn't want to pay $700 for sealant. So before I would start my shift I at the grocery store I walked around the huge parking lot and put flyers on cars, especially if they were brand new and still had the paper dealer plates. My flyer said, "The dealership was trying to charge me $700 for sealant. I can do it for $195. If you have two cars, I would do it for $295." I started getting phone calls. It was amazing.

I started hiring some of the box boys from the grocery store. I would give them each a gallon of sealant, set up appointments and make sure they did a nice job and the customers were happy.

Business was going so well that I ordered more sealant by the cases. I would fill up 6 oz. plastic bottles, make up some tags and started selling those. It was my first white label product.

I knew at a very young age that I was going to be an entrepreneur. I didn't want to work for somebody else. I saw how hard my parents worked, how they were in constant fear of getting laid off when the economy slowed down. To me, it left a lasting impression, and I didn't want to count on somebody else, I wanted to be the person in charge and responsible for my future.

My long-term girlfriend and school friends knew that I marched to the beat of a different drummer, but they thought I was a crazy, lazy, dreamer. I don't blame them. They were brought up to go to college, find a good job, and get married. That was their growing up experience. Mine was different.

Luckily, my parents were always encouraging and wanted me to do something that I would enjoy. They never held me back and never said anything negative. They were the best.

LESSONS LEARNED

My car sealant business went really well… for about a year. Then I noticed it was slowing down. I found out that a lot of guys I hired to help me were going out on their own. I can't blame them, they saw the money coming and figured, "Okay, this is easy, I can do it on my own."

That was a big lesson for me. I learned that you have to be careful when you train and teach people your business, you could be creating your own competition.

That business taught me to keep my eyes and ears open and to notice opportunities as they became available.

Ever since I was young, I wanted to get into real estate. I noticed people who owned rental homes, made money. I always thought this could be a way for me to travel the world and live off the rent.

I opened my real estate appraisal business about 26 years ago. I had five appraisers that I trained working for me. It was great. I would sit behind the desk, schedule their appointments and review their work. It was a good way of making money. Then I expanded into mortgage lending. Both businesses were making six figures, which gave me the opportunity to travel around the world.

All I needed was an Internet connection and e-mail. I worked from my laptop and my clients had no idea that I was out of the country. I was married; my wife was a real estate agent and also my business partner. It had worked out well... I thought.

In 2008, the real estate market collapsed. Both my wife and I got slammed when the market collapsed. Our monopoly board of rental homes and living off the rent was falling apart. Before I knew it, my marriage started falling apart as well.

I became a one-person shop for the both the appraisal and mortgage companies. I had to lay off all my employees. I fell into a small depression. It was just a horribly sad time.

I think it made me a stronger person because when I hit rock bottom, I thought, the only way that this is going to get better is by looking up. It's hard to imagine something positive could from this, but it did.

I closed the appraisal shop and focused on generating leads for my struggling mortgage business. It turns out I was pretty good at. I was able cherry pick the mortgage leads that I wanted to work with, and other mortgage lenders would buy a lot of the leads I didn't want.

At one point, mortgage financing got extremely tough. I was fighting with the lenders and the underwriters because I was having a hard time even getting loan approvals on the leads I had cherry picked.

Then I thought other mortgage companies might have better luck, so I decided just to sell all of the leads I was generating.

That's when I found out that I could make just as much money in lead generation, using the Internet and e-mail. Slowly but surely I knew I wanted to start something that could help people. It made me feel good about myself, and it made me a stronger person.

It was also the beginning of the marketing agency I run today.

BACK TO THE START:
Advice to My Pre-Entrepreneur Self

If I could give one piece of advice to my pre-entrepreneur self, it would be to find niche or hobby that you enjoy. Then see if you can teach or share it with others. Then see if you can be compensated or rewarded for it. I don't just mean monetarily, look for a big smile or thank you.

Have your eyes and ears open. Look for problems that businesses are having and help them find a solution.

Helping others is what helped me.

About Patrick Mejia

Patrick Mejia currently owns his own marketing agency offering free advice to older business owners that are not up-to-date with current marketing strategies.

He helps his prospects understand what their competitors are doing and why it is working for them. He will then show his clients how to combat their advertising tactics to increase their customer base and become more competitive. He offers personalized packages that suit the affordability of each client.

When Patrick is not helping others expand their business, he can be found on the beach. He has been teaching adult volleyball for over 18 years. He has found that meeting new people in a non-threatening environment allows him to gain potential clients trust. Patrick loves the outdoors and takes time to enjoy the scenery before moving on.

Ambrose Digital Agency

WESBSITE
AmbroseDigitalAgency.com

EMAIL
info@AmbroseDigitalAgency.com

PHONE
310-504-2747

DANIEL GIORDANO

THE START: Journey To Entrepreneurship

I had the entrepreneurial bug at a young age. My dad had a part-time painting business and from the time I was about eight years old, he would yank me out of bed on the weekends to go to work with him doing little odd jobs here and there.

I always came up with creative ways to create cash. I would buy popsicles and re-sell them on the corner in the summertime, rake and bag leaves in the fall, shovel snow during the winter and everything in between.

During my transition from college, I worked for one of the largest painting companies of it's kind in the Philadelphia area. That job taught me a lot about what I did NOT want to do. I also learned to recognize my value. I was about nineteen, and they wanted to pay me minimum wage to start. The guy interviewing me said, "I'll start you off at seven bucks an hour." I came back with, "Tell you what; I will work for free for two weeks. At the end of the two weeks, I'm going to walk in here, and I'm going to tell you what you are going to pay me. If you don't like me after two weeks, then you don't owe me anything."

Two weeks later I walked in and said, "I want twenty dollars an hour." He agreed, and by the time I left, one year later, I was making thirty-six dollars an hour. They didn't want me to leave, but I knew that I needed to start my own thing. There was a lot more for me out there, and I wanted to be in control of my future.

CROSSING OVER:
From "I'm going to be" to "I am" an Entrepreneur

My biggest desire was to be able to do something that I enjoyed, and the first thing I fell into was the painting industry. I liked Victorian and historic homes, so I decided, to focus on that. I wound up building my first company around restoring historic homes. In less than three years it was the largest company of it's kind in the area, and I had over twenty employees. I had a lot of fun because I was focusing on something that I really enjoyed doing, which was important to m then, and still is today.

Even after I sold that Company in 1998 and moved to South Florida, I wound up falling right back into the painting industry.

I remember like it was yesterday, I was working in a ten million dollar home and having a conversation with the owner. I always asked these people what they did for a living and how they created this ultra-level of success. I remember looking out at the ocean and saying, "Something's got to change. I need to do something different."

Some magical things happened since moving to Florida. One, I had my first child and then I had my second child. I remember thinking, "I want to be the dad who is going to be home with my kids. I don't want to be out of the house twelve to sixteen hours a day." I wanted to be able to spend quality time with them. I didn't want just to see them bright and early in the morning and at night. I wanted to be part of their lives.

I realized that I had to do some things differently. That meant no more big contracts. It also meant downsizing, and I'd already built the business up to needing employees again. The motivating factor for me was the family and being able to create the lifestyle that I wanted so that I could be home with my kids and my wife.

The rest of my family thought I was crazy. They always have, even to this day I hear, "Why don't you go get a nice, safe, secure job and settle and live like everybody else?"

Obviously, I was at a point where I was doing my own thing, helping to raise my family when I realized that it's up to me, and I don't care if they are supporting me or not. I would have liked their support, but I was not going to wait for it. The interesting thing is after I became successful they shifted their thinking and said, "Oh, well, it must be nice. It happened overnight."

They forgot the years in between of plugging away trying to figure things out. I had been working hard at it. I definitely did not have total family support but my immediate family, my wife, has always been supportive in everything I have done.

There was a period of struggling to figure out what was going to bring the money in when I stumbled into the affiliate marketing world, and I literally mean STUMBLED into it.

I started dabbling in 1999 and figured out how to get blacklisted by my Internet service provider because I did not know I couldn't email people from the inbox that they were emailing me from. I figured out how to get banned and blacklisted by eBay and Amazon as well. I figured out all the wrong things to do.

It was not that I was doing anything illegal, it was just simple things, and I didn't know any better. It was a huge learning experience for me to discover what to do and what not to do. I have had to struggle through to be able to create what I wanted in my life.

In 2001 everything shifted for me when I realized that I could make money online and transition from having to be out on the construction site that I was working in as a painter. It was a revelation when that reality hit. I would never have to pick up a paintbrush again.

I was able to create income online with no products and very limited knowledge. I knew how to search the Internet and pretty much check email at that time, but I was still able to create a multiple six figure a year income from that.

Of course, I had all of the struggles and "What if's" you can think of when it's your first time doing something. "What if they don't pay me?" but then… I remember like it was yesterday, $5,468.00 was wired into my account. I said, "This is real," and within thirty days the next payment came and it was over $29,000.00. What an amazing experience. I realized that I could write my own ticket.

LESSONS LEARNED

Keep it simple. That is the biggest lesson that I have learned over the years because we tend to make our lives way more complex than they need to be.

It always comes down to the basic fundamentals. If somebody is looking for a product or service that you have to offer, how can you position yourself to get your link, your website, your product and service in front of them before your competitor?

A lot of times we get caught up in the shiny object syndrome that's out there, including me. Saying, "Oh, this looks cool. I wonder how I could use this." It still comes down to building a relationship between you and the client by providing them with a quality product at good that value.

The biggest lessons I've learned through past failures in business is from bringing on partners. Everything needs to be clearly spelled out before getting involved in any venture. Be clear from the very beginning and have a strategy in place, because eventually, a partner is going to want to leave or something is going to change. When you know and agree upfront about what to do when that happens, and then it's great.

BACK TO THE START:
Advice to My Pre-Entrepreneur Self

You can't look back and say should have, could have, or would have because it's a waste of time. Listen to your intuition. When you get that gut feeling about whether something is good or bad or the right time to take a next step or risk, go with it and trust your intuition. You have that for a reason.

About Daniel Giordano

Daniel is a hard-working man that puts 100% effort into everything he does. He believes that a successful business could not be completed without giving it your all. He has come from a humble beginning of painting houses as a child with his father on the weekends and growing up to establish his own Internet business. Currently, Daniel is committed to his company, his family, and his faith. He believes in always going the extra mile to support charities that benefit life around him.

Nature is his second home. He can be found rock climbing, scuba diving, golfing, and practicing martial arts with his kids. He is proud that three of his children are black belts; the fourth is too young to start his karate career.

Daniel Giordano

WESBSITE
DanielGiordano.com

CHRIS DALEY

THE START: Journey to Entrepreneurship

I was born on the Island of Jamaica and migrated with my parents to the United States. We lived with relatives on a farm, but I didn't take to farm life. I had a hunger for books. In the summertime, when I needed to be in the field, I'd hide in trees with my books to study. I had that thirst for knowledge and a desire to do something with it.

During high school, I remember clearly in physics class learning about electricity. I marveled at how the conduction of electricity happened. We didn't even have electricity where I lived at the time. Shortly after this, when electricity came to my neighborhood, I offered to help some of the neighbors replace the wiring in their houses. I didn't know that the gauge of the wire mattered and replaced their wires, which were actually of a greater gauge, with the same wire from my physics lab.

In the middle of the night, their lights were going out, and they were pretty upset, but I was able to restore their electricity. I learned about customer relationship when things go bad with a client.

One summer my brother Mike and I got a pair of walkie-talkies. We wanted people in the community to experience this high technology, so we decided to set up a business and charge them to talk on our walkie-talkies. Right then, I knew that if I have a technology that can add value to the quality of lives, then I could make a difference.

I studied electrical engineering and went to work for the Research & Development Center for Bell Labs, which was renowned for its patents and went on to do microchip designs. After about ten years, I started to feel that the engineering was not as satisfying as I would like.

I became interested in marketing when I was working on a project that saved one of the designs within our system. This guy said, "Look, you come work for me, and I will teach you everything you need to know about marketing. You know engineering. I think you have some marketing DNA in you. Come with me and I will teach you everything you need to know about marketing."

I took him up on the offer, and we had a great time. This was back in the days when DSL was the hot connection technology.

We were able to take a small startup from $6 million up to $365 million worth of product. Then came the burst of the tech bubble. A lot of the startup guys got wiped out, and there I was without any clients in the telecommunications marketing space.

CROSSING OVER:
From "I'm going to be" to "I am" an Entrepreneur

I decided to start my own marketing agency and made an investment in a franchised marketing system. I didn't do the needed due diligence and didn't fully understand the technology or the customer side of it so I simply could not get off the ground. It was a pretty expensive lesson. I had to move on from that and get some more stable income, so I went to work for a government agency. Taking that job allowed me to prove myself and gave me enough flexibility to be able to restart my marketing agency.

I had worked for a corporation for so long, and I didn't want my destiny to be locked into that kind of single stream of income. Knowing that in a high-tech job with that kind of technical background, I could lose my job and that would not be a comfortable situation. I wanted to be able to provide for myself and use my skills outside of that. I said, "I will never put myself in a situation where I depend on a job for my sustenance."

I wanted to make sure I would do what I needed to maintain my situation, to be commendable and perform to my ability, but all my extra energies would not be used to make money for somebody else. It would be to make money for myself, and a legacy for my children. My corporate ambition was limited to doing my best without climbing another corporate career ladder. All of my investments and passion were poured into starting my marketing agency.

Now I focus on small businesses and professionals that can't afford a big marketing agency or full-time staff. My agency helps them with marketing and reputation. If they have the means of making a difference in the community, I want to be there to make sure that the community knows about them, and they can have a sustained presence in that community as opposed to being knocked off by a large enterprise that may not have the same kind of vested interest in that community.

I had a very supportive family. Becoming a single parent with three girls, I was fortunate to have a natural supportive environment with my brothers, sisters, and mom around me.

My brother was in the technology field and had made that leap outside of a corporate environment. I could lean on his seasoned experience. He was a little more cautious than I am so I would bounce ideas off him to see if it was out of the box but still sustainable. He has probably been my major advisor because he understands technology and knows where it's going.

LESSONS LEARNED

I learned that technology is neat, sexy. It can mesmerize you, but you have to follow the entire value chain to see what kind of marketplace you are playing in. You need to know how it's received by your clients and customers and how they value it. It is important to understand how they are going to adopt what you really bring to the marketplace.

You can't just say "Gee, everybody is going to want one of these." You need to make sure that it has a sustaining business model behind it, and is not just a flash in the pan.

I learned that you need to really understand the entire ecosystem of your business; it's more than just the technological offering you have. If you don't understand it and if you don't have resources to fund that, you must be very careful or look for other places or partnerships to be able to do that.

Make sure that you set up a system that you know is sustaining. If it's beyond yourself, knowing what kinds of partnerships you have with other people or stakeholders to make that work is vital. That's the lesson learned that I take away: Look at all the stakeholders from yourself to the clients to the technology to the regulations. If you don't have visibility into all of that, it could come back to bite you.

BACK TO THE START:
Advice to My Pre-Entrepreneur Self

Don't be dazzled by technology. Look at the entire picture. It is easy to run up a shiny object because they can paint a pretty picture. Understanding the human factor is critical; how people adopt technology to make it a part of their lives.

About Chris Daley

Chris Daley lives in Silver Spring, Maryland with his lovely wife, Joy. He has four fabulous daughters and three grandkids, Hallie, John and Isabella.

He founded Digital2Grow, LLC where he helps clients build five-star reputations. He also helps them drive traffic to their offerings and implement funnel systems to add automation smarts to realize maximum conversion. Clients can also build their market leadership position through his authority branding formulae.

Chris can be found listening to audiobooks while traveling to one of his many charity events. One of his favorites is helping to educate young men to get them interested in pursuing a higher education and giving back to their community. He is also involved in a nonprofit center that focuses on helping homeless single mothers find homes.

Digital2Grow LLC

WEBSITE
Digital2GrowMedia.com

FACEBOOK
Facebook.com/Chris.Daley1

EMAIL
chris@digital2growllc.com

TWITTER
@chrisdaley

LINKEDIN
LinkedIn.com/in/ChrisDaley56

VANESSA LAMARO
AND MARY MARTIN

THE START: Journey To Entrepreneurship

Vanessa Lamaro: I never saw myself as an employee. I was one of five kids, and both of my parents were self-employed. With the exception of one, all of my siblings went into their own businesses.

As a teenager, I knew I would not be someone who had a job working for someone else. I just remember being extremely miserable at the couple of jobs I had. It went against my grain. As I was walking through a pharmacy recently I looked at all the women working there, and I thought, "Oh my God, it would kill my soul to be in here 9-5, Monday thru Friday." I worked like that as a 19-year-old, and I remember Monday morning feeling miserable and Friday afternoon feeling elated. That pain was the catalyst for me. I don't have that anymore.

I'm an information and education junkie. I love learning, so during this time I started to do a lot of self-development work. I absorbed what Anthony Robbins taught in his seminars learning and improving both myself as a person and also in business. The types of people that I've learned from always tend to inspire others to become something greater. I think if you're constantly consuming that kind of information on a daily basis, you really have no other option than to reach for something higher than having a job.

Mary Martin: Unlike Vanessa, who is much more of a visionary, I followed the crowds in my earlier years when I was working. I did not see myself as an entrepreneur. Now I can't see anything but that. My father always went to work, and that was the model for me growing up.

I love working with people and have always been drawn to jobs helping people solve problems. But once I became a naturopath and started seeing patients I realized that every hour I spent with somebody was the only way I would get paid. I didn't have a lot of extra money even though I was putting in all the time that I had. There were no other hours in the day to for me to make more and if people canceled or changed their appointments I wouldn't have as much money that week.

A lot of people burn out in this industry from seeing patients non-stop. I thought, "This is crazy; I cannot live like this. I want to have some freedom in my life, I want to have some choices in the decisions that I can make and I don't want it to be governed by dollars." I began learning Internet marketing as I was looking for different ways to make passive income.

CROSSING OVER:
From "I'm going to be" to "I am" an Entrepreneur

Mary Martin: I moved from Canada to Australia and did not quite figure out what I wanted to do. I didn't fit into any jobs or any education experience I had here. I had a marketing degree, so I decided to start an adventure wear clothing company where I designed and made the clothes.

At the time Australia had an opportunity through government grants and loans. I had to put together a lot of information and a lot of projections, a business plan, connections and that. I got that approved and got a grant and a loan for a year. I just went for it. I didn't know anything about selling clothes.

I learned a lot of things through the Government Incentive Program. It was quite a structured program, and then I took a business course. I learned more marketing and just kind of went for it. I wound up selling to 21 stores around Australia; it went quite well.

I ended up selling the business and moved to Korea for three years to teach English. At that time I knew I wanted to come back and study to be a Naturopath. That was my first experience in entrepreneurship. I got a taste for it and an inkling that I could do anything that I set my mind on.

Vanessa Lamaro: My first entrepreneurial venture was with a girlfriend. We opened up a beauty salon where we offered body treatments, massage, waxing, and nails along with all the regular beauty treatments.

The business was a success. We had a great following, and I would consider that more of a small business venture. It is entrepreneurial, but I think what we have our sights on now is much grander. At that time, I was still working in the business, and we potentially could have optimized it so that we became more managerial. The way I consider entrepreneurship is a little bit more forward thinking. It's taking a risk.

Mary Martin: Our current company is called The Baby Builders. It solves a problem that has gone international: it's for couples that are having challenges conceiving a baby. 1 in 6 couples now having trouble conceiving a baby. In our role as Naturopaths, we specialize in fertility health. We have set up our international online business to offer services and products that help people educate themselves with consultations as well as herbal and nutritional medicine to help overcome different various fertility challenges.

Vanessa Lamaro: We no longer work one-on-one with patients in this capacity, but we now are more overseeing the business and are involved in generating business. It's gone from a consultant role into more of a managerial and marketing role, but with a lot more freedom involved. We no longer swap hours for money. Because it's an online business, really the amount that we could make for one minute is exponential. We could sell one e-book, or we could sell 1,000 e-books.

In a small business, or in a job, there's no way we could have that kind of leverage. It's a powerful, powerful model.

Mary Martin: When we started this I think there was some speculation from people of "Oh an online business. Right, like that has not been done before. Can you make money online?" Most people don't want to put their time, money and effort into that. I think there has been more skepticism because we are about four years in a pre-launch mode for this project. We haven't done it quickly. I think a lot of people thought we were nuts, many still do, and we are out to prove the naysayers wrong.

Vanessa Lamaro: I think the naysayers give us more fire in our bellies. They give us more motivation to prove everyone wrong. I can't say that is a super positive way to live life, but it does inspire us. It shows that we have worked hard and have what it takes to facilitate the project's success. I would say because my family members are self-employed they thought it was a crazy idea. I definitely have had people in my life that are a lot more conservative and have said that they think it is a risky idea or that they think it is a bad idea. I do not listen to them, so it is not much of an issue.

LESSONS LEARNED

Mary Martin: We've learned to choose the people we surround ourselves with wisely. We choose our team of experts with great care. Our biggest challenge is outsourcing: finding people who know what they are doing, charging the right price, giving the right times and not getting ripped off.

Vanessa Lamaro: I would say what I would do differently before jumping in boots and all is really be quite methodical in making sure that you've got all the pieces to your business puzzle. We signed up for a lot of our plug-ins that cost us quite a lot on a monthly basis probably earlier than we should have before we started making money. There were probably some things we should have done before we did those.

BACK TO THE START:
Advice to My Pre-Entrepreneur Self

Mary Martin: Nobody is doing it the way you're doing it. Find your angles, find the way your point of difference as to how you're going to position yourself, try it and go for it. Line yourself up with good people, get yourself organized, and put yourself out there.

Vanessa Lamaro: Make sure you've got all your ducks in a row, all your content, your website sorted before you go investing in some other things that could be invested in at a later point of the business.

About Mary Martin and Vanessa Lamaro

Mary and Vanessa are co-owners of *The Baby Builders.* Both have ventured off into their unique line of work before coming together. Devoting their lives to helping others is their passion. They have dedicated over four years to produce the most informative and up-to-date information to help couples who are having a hard time getting pregnant. Helping couples regain their fertility mojo is their number one goal.

The Baby Builders

WEBSITE
TheBabyBuilders.com

BRIAN HOWER

THE START: Journey To Entrepreneurship

As a child, I split my focus between being a baseball player and a doctor. I grew up pretty poor. My dad was a blue-collar worker, and our family struggled financially. I sold lemonade and that kind of thing, like the rest of the kids did, but I wasn't thinking about business at all.

I was a good student all my life, but when I went to college for pre-med, it was a lot harder. Working full-time to pay for my books, clothes, or McDonald's once in a while, just trying to survive as a college kid was pretty ambitious, and I was struggling the whole time. It got to the point that I was just trying to at least get my degree so I'd have a chance in life.

By the time I graduated with my Bachelor's degree I was too exhausted to go to medical school, and I needed money something fierce, so I took a position as a chemist.

I wasn't thinking about being an entrepreneur at all, just trying to get some traction. It wasn't until I was actually in the working world that I figured out, "Uh oh, I'm not going to make enough money to do what I want to do." That was my first clue that I needed to do something more.

I remember driving around the neighborhood and seeing people with bigger, nicer houses than I had. I looked at the paycheck from my chemist job and thought, "How do they have that house? I'll never be able to afford that based on what I'm making." I guess as an entrepreneur you have to have a desire for more. I don't want to call it greed. It's almost like a measuring stick. I'm worth more than what I've achieved so far. I always had the feeling that there's more in me.

It's not just about making life easier for myself. A big motivation is knowing the better I do, the more I can do for someone else. I can help my son or daughter, even a neighbor. I want to be able to inspire friends who are struggling. I started to realize a job probably wasn't going to allow me to do that.

CROSSING OVER:
From "I'm going to be" to "I am" an Entrepreneur

I was working for one of those phonebook companies that starts with the word "Yellow" selling advertising and websites. I did a lot of research and learned about websites and the Internet, and I knew that most of the small business activity was going to move into that the direction. I figured out that what I was selling for this company was not enough. The websites were just an ad on the Internet, with a picture and some paragraphs. But then enough people have to stumble across that ad, and maybe it will influence them, maybe it will motivate them to call, but probably not. People won't find it just because it's there, at least not enough to build any real sales or any business.

There were a lot of mergers in the industry and that pretty much left me without a job. That lack of stability and control over my income or career is what motivated me to start my own business. I said, "The heck with this. I'm going to do my thing and try to make a go of it."

I wouldn't say I was an entrepreneur until I started my current company, Searchlight Business Advocates, by giving it a name, doing business ads, and registering with the state of Pennsylvania. It was at that point that I said, "Now what? I need to get customers to have a business and make some money." That's when I got my first ever client. I think they paid me $50 a month; almost nothing, but I was so excited thinking, "Oh my gosh, I'm in business!"

It was hardly any money, but somebody was paying me, and that meant that others would too. That's the moment I knew that I could really do this. I was a businessperson.

A lot of my family and friends were totally baffled because they didn't understand what I was even doing. I've tried to explain it, and they still don't understand, but now I think they are interested. So many people are in that "I've got to work a job" mindset. It's the American way. It's a different person to think, "I want more, I can do more" and have the confidence and willingness to take the risk to get more. My wife didn't know whether to give me credit for what I've accomplished or to think I'm a fool for spending nine years chasing 'The Dream.' Now it's more than a dream because people are paying me. It's a business!

It is scary, but I did it.

LESSONS LEARNED

I've learned a couple of important lessons. One is when you prospect, the worst thing you can do is sound like a sales person. You have to be genuine, and you have to be sincerely trying to help the client. I think that's what almost all salespeople do wrong. They think, "I have to sell and persuade and convince." That's the wrong approach.

You have to call and be genuine, almost off the cuff. "I don't know if I can help you, but I think I have something that might be of benefit to you. This is what I do. What do you think?" The whole lesson is you have to get the conversation started. If you come off as a sales person, that brick wall or that gate goes up, and you're done right there.

The second thing is don't sell yourself short. I've had 60 clients and the first 50 of them were minnows, and I should have been going after the whales. (Maybe not whales, but dolphins.) I went after the minnows. That cost me a lot of money, but it also enabled me to learn a lot.

Cold calling and cold emailing, getting no response or getting shut down, that's hard. That's the worst part, and it is probably why people don't want to be in business. They don't want to experience any failure. You have to find a way to be more effective. I'll never call ten people and not get hung up on by one of them, or be treated rudely by one of them. It's just part of the process.

BACK TO THE START:
Advice to My Pre-Entrepreneur Self

You shouldn't be focused on helping yourself first. Find something that will help others first. If it's only about you, then you will fail. If it's about others, then you have a business concept.

About Brian Hower

Brian Hower is and will always be a self-made man. He never gives up even when people are telling him to give up and find a "normal" job. He loves the career he has created for himself and his family. It allows him to keep up his hobby of gardening while being able to spend time with his two sons and daughter. By running his own business, Searchlight Business Advocates, Brian is able to enjoy one of the small pleasures like taking casual drives to the beach to get his mind off work.

The endless support of his wife and family pushes Brian to strive to find new clientele and expand his business of building unlimited copy, social media, and video for the web. It's e-commerce to the nth degree, which results in a high amount of traffic, completely targeted, and researched. It becomes a virtual business on the Internet, much like a business with a physical address.

Now you have your street business and your Internet business, or you could have one or the other. They work together. I call it a clone of physical businesses because everything that can be done at the store can be done from the computer at the virtual store. That is what I build for people, and that's why they pay me because it is a real business.

WEBSITE
Business-Internet-and-Media.com

FACEBOOK
Facebook.com/Searchlight-Business-Advocates-149313115123501/

www.ingramcontent.com/pod-product-compliance
Lightning Source LLC
Chambersburg PA
CBHW050510210326
41521CB00011B/2394